# Islam

# Islam

## An Introduction for Christians

*Paul Varo Martinson, Editor*
*Translated by Stefanie Ormsby Cox*

**Augsburg**
MINNEAPOLIS

ISLAM: AN INTRODUCTION FOR CHRISTIANS

Translation of *Was jeder vom Islam wissen muss*, copyright 1990 Gütersloher Verlagshaus Gerd Mohn. First published by the United Evangelical Lutheran Church of Germany and the Evangelical Church in Germany. Two chapters relevant to the German context have been deleted and a new section on Islam in North America has been added.

Excerpts from *The Qur'an* are reprinted from *The Meaning of The Holy Qur'an* (new revised edition), copyright © 1989 A. C. Amana Corporation. Used by permission.

Scripture quotations are from the New Revised Standard Version Bible, copyright © 1989 by the Division of Christian Education of the National Council of the Churches of Christ in the United States of America. Used with permission.

Cover design: Ann Elliot Artz Hadland
Interior design: Karen Buck

Library of Congress Cataloging-in-Publication Data
[Was jeder vom Islam wissen muss. German.]
    Islam : an introduction for Christians / Paul Varo Martinson,
editor : translated by Stefanie O. Cox. — 1st English-language ed.
      p.    cm.
    Translation of: Was jeder vom Islam wissen muss.
    Includes bibliographical references and index.
    ISBN 0-8066-2583-X
    1. Islam—Relations—Christianity.   2. Christianity and other
religions—Islam.   3. Islam.     I. Martinson, Paul Varo, 1934–
II. Cox, Stefanie O.   III. Title.
BP172.W2615     1994
297'.0242—dc20                                                    94-2356
                                                                    CIP

The paper used in this publication meets the minimum requirements of American National Standard for Information Sciences—Permanence of Paper for Printed Library Materials, ANSI Z329.48-1984.                                        ∞™

Manufactured in the U.S.A.                                        AF 9-2583

                                          6    7    8    9    10

# Contents

# Editor's Preface

The purpose of this book is to inform the Christian community concerning the faith of Muslims who dwell in our midst. Although this material was originally prepared for a European context and audience, it is material that is also very useful for a North American audience in which Islam is a growing presence. To be sure, there are differences between the Muslim community here and that in Europe. For instance, in North America we do not have a predominantly Turkish immigrant community as Germany does, and educational and professional reasons have played a larger role than labor opportunities in drawing Muslim immigrants to North America. We are grateful, nevertheless, to our German friends for this practical and informative text, which can be of great help to us.

I also wish to express appreciation for the work of the translator, Stefanie Ormsby Cox. The text came to me already translated, for which I am grateful. Jonathan Case, a doctoral candidate at Luther Seminary, has been of immense help in working through this text once again. Mr. Case has at many points compared the text closely with the original German. We have had a few basic principles in mind in the work of editing, including clarity and consistency in the text. At times we have felt at liberty to render the translation rather freely, whether eliding or amplifying with a few words as the case might be. At a few points we have modified or slightly nuanced the theological formulations for the sake of theological clarity, especially at points where Scripture, the Trinity, or the incarnation has been the focus of discussion.

One major change from the original German is the dropping of the extensive sections called "documentation" after each chapter. For a North American audience it seemed that these extended citations might need further interpretation to have the intended impact. By dropping them, the text also spoke more directly. Some of the appendices have been reworked or replaced. The bibliography has been completely redone—a German bibliography was hardly relevant. We have also been more selective in the bibliography listed. The chronology has been somewhat reworked. We have also attempted to standardize the foreign terms used, avoiding Turkish terms in preference for the Arabic. We have not used the diacritical markings in most cases, however, assuming their use to be overly esoteric for a general audience. The standard for the Arabic forms used was a system of transliteration common to many standard English reference works, such as the *New Encyclopaedia Brittanica*. Wherever possible we conformed to this. We also referred to such works as *The Encyclopedia of Religion*, *The Concise Encyclopedia of Islam*, and *The Encyclopaedia of Islam*, both old and new editions. Quotations from the Qur'an are from the Yusuf Ali translation.

Finally, a section on Islam in North America has been added. This, for obvious reasons, seemed a necessary addition. While there is literature available on this subject—upon which this section has been completely dependent—it is not necessarily readily accessible to the readers of this book. In fact, the study of Islam in North America appears to be at the point of an explosive take-off. Much will be appearing in the years ahead. For this reason we have included in the bibliography on Islam in North America a good deal of the standard material already available as well as a few items that are of very recent vintage or await publication in the near future. Those interested will have a good basis from which to begin their further explorations on this subject.

Finally, I wish also to express my appreciation for the several reviewers of the manuscript, especially Professor Amin Kader, for their helpful comments. The hard and careful work of the editors, Irene Getz, Lois Torvik, and Sheryl Strauss has been simply essential.

We trust that our communities of faith will be well served by making this material available.

PAUL VARO MARTINSON

# Foreword
# from the German Edition

Since June of 1982 when the first pamphlet on the topic "Qur'an" in the German series "Information Islam" appeared, nearly four million have been distributed in Germany. This clearly demonstrates the existence of an enormous need for factual information on the Islamic faith. There are clear reasons for this need.

About 1.8 million people in Germany either confess the Islamic faith or belong to the intellectual and cultural tradition of the Islamic world. For western Europe as a whole the total is more than 6 million. For the most part they arrived as "guest workers" from Turkey, North Africa, the Indian subcontinent, and elsewhere. Subsequently they gained immigrant status and began to form cultural and religious minorities within an increasingly pluralistic European society. Eventually they will take their place within the European household. We do well, therefore, to become acquainted with our Muslim neighbors, however foreign their life-style, attitudes, and faith might seem to us.

With the outbreak of the controversy surrounding Salman Rushdie's *Satanic Verses,* many who advocate liberality and tolerance toward Muslim minorities in the West were shocked by the harshness and severity with which Muslims defended Islam against this—as they perceived it—blasphemous attack. The image of an aggressive and fanatical Islam, which people in the West have carried with them for centuries and which has been reinforced by media images in recent years, was confirmed. Is this the true face of Islam? Or can one rather speak of a very different Islam, one that leads to a gentle, upright, generous, and open spirit? What is Islam really like? Which image corresponds to reality and which reflects our prejudices? We need to learn more.

For Christians it is especially important to know about Islam. Islam has always claimed to confess the true faith in the only God, the creator of heaven and earth. This is the same faith in God that Christians were intended to hold, but, according to Muslims, they now fail to see clearly due to errors and adulterations that have crept into their teachings. Are we Christians ready to discuss and respond to this claim? Do we know our own faith well enough to be accountable for it, and do we know the faith of Muslims well enough to make meaningful judgments in our conversation? Christians and Muslims can make many faith statements in common; they can do many things together in obedience to God's command. Encounters with each other can bring them closer together. Yet, at the same time, they continue to experience a mutual foreignness that cannot be overcome and that clearly stems from the central declarations of their faiths. To get beyond the superficial, people must be well acquainted and know a great deal about each other.

Only in an encounter that relies on mutual understanding and respect does the faith to which Christians witness have a chance to be comprehended by Muslims. This is especially true in a context such as Germany, where Christians comprise the majority, are close to the centers of power, and enjoy more societal privileges than Muslims. The latter are a minority and almost all foreigners. As such they are subject to harsh attitudes, discrimination, and enmity. The witness to faith in Jesus Christ, in whom Christians find truth and salvation, can only be convincing when we deal fairly with others in their life situation. But how can we be fair when we have so little understanding of their faith?

Thus there are many reasons to seek information about Islam. A series of pamphlets was designed by the United Evangelical Lutheran Church of Germany (UELCG) in 1981 to meet this need.

The goal of this volume is similar: to provide information about our Muslim neighbors' faith. The series was arranged in a logical order and further expanded to become this book. The German title is *What Everyone Should Know About Islam*. The book is intended not only to provoke, but even more to entice one to read, to reference, and to use. Some will remember the title *Judaism: An Introduction for Christians*, first published in German and later in English. That book was prepared in response to a great demand for information about Judaism. A similar demand was one of the reasons the UELCG decided to begin a further series about another great religion that affects the Western world.

The work group, called together by the Church Council of the UELCG and which is responsible for the content, brought together theologians, specialists, practical experts, and academicians. One of the working principles from the outset was that no pamphlet would be produced that was not first reviewed by several Muslim scholars. Their comments and corrections were usually taken into account. In addition every attempt was made to be true to the claim set forth in the title, and to offer factual, carefully prepared, and objectively presented information about Islam. A special effort was also made to keep the language clear and readily understandable. The church office of the Evangelical Church in Germany (ECG) joined the UELCG in publishing this book in order to reach as broad a church audience as possible.

Ulrich Dietzfelbinger, special assistant to the Church College in Berlin Zehlendorf, edited the pamphlet series for the book edition. His work included the collection and selection of the documents, the preparation of chronologies, lists, and indices, as well as the content-appropriate arrangement of the text. Thanks to him for this editorial work!

# Introduction:
# Everyday Encounters between Christians and Muslims

Even though Muslims have been living among us for many years, today there are still many first encounters between Christians and Muslims. Families follow relatives, coming to Europe and North America from their home countries. Each new encounter between faithful Christians and Muslims, or between fully secular-thinking Christians and Muslims, carries with it the possibility of being an enriching success or a hardening failure. Much is required to prevent failure: goodwill, patience, tact, politeness, and respect. This is particularly the case when things seem strange, peculiar, or objectionable. Successful encounter requires genuine interest in the other person, willingness and ability to share information about oneself and one's traditions, and openness to being questioned. Of course the most important ingredient is to accept and treat the other person as an individual on equal terms: as a person with a personal history, with personal hopes and expectations, with personal fears and hurts.

It is often the little things, however, that make the first contact unnecessarily difficult for both sides. Here are some helpful suggestions.

Different customs can easily lead to misunderstanding during a first encounter in the hallway. For example, in Germany when a man greets a new Turkish neighbor, the woman may not respond but quickly retreat into her apartment. This does not signify any rejection, but is simply behavior consistent with a conservative religious attitude. Private contacts hardly exist between Muslim men and women who are not of the same family. It is the woman's duty to her family to be restrained; a man shows respect to a woman and her family by refraining from talking with her.

In other areas, too, the relationship between the genders is handled with great caution among Muslims: Girls are often not permitted to participate in physical education at school, especially swimming; class trips that include both boys and girls are rarely possible; it is always the exception for girls from strict Islamic families to go to parties that include boys. Such behaviors should not be criticized and rejected out of hand. They serve to protect the Islamic tradition in an environment experienced as strange and often unfriendly.

The greeting ceremony depends on how well people know each other. At the beginning of a friendship a handshake is appropriate. Between men and women, however, it is often limited to a *"merhaba,"* a verbal "hello." Some have the custom, when better acquainted, of greeting one another with a double kiss on the cheeks. Youth express their respect toward elders by brushing the outstretched hand of the elder with their lips and forehead.

It is also a good idea to make certain things clear about personal visits and invitations to dinner. For instance, when entering a Muslim home, people take their shoes off and the hosts offer slippers. In some cases, a non-Muslim woman invited to dinner will eat with the men, but often the hostess will serve everyone and then eat by herself afterward in the kitchen. After the meal women and men generally converse separately. However, customs will vary from one culture to another.

In a Muslim's home, formulas of prayer in which the name "Allah" is used are often heard; for example, at the beginning of the meal. These include the *basmalah,* "in the name of God"; the *istithna,* "as God wills"; the *hamdala,* "Praise belongs to God"; and the *masallah,* "God has willed it." The Islamic tradition is not shy about using the name of God frequently, even in relationship to ordinary events, although no religious meaning may be apparent. Muslims understand such use as an expression of the fact that a person's entire life should be subject to the will of God. For example, the *basmalah* is spoken at the start of each new activity—the start of a trip, entering a car, and so on; the *istithna* accompanies every declaration about plans and goals in the near future and the long-term future; the *hamdala* is often given as a response to the query, How are you?; the *masallah* expresses amazement, surprise, as well as good wishes—for example, when visiting a newborn child (and its parents) for the first time. The actual Islamic greeting is *as-salamu alaykum*, "Peace be with you," which is answered *wa alaykum-as-salam* "and upon you be peace."

If one invites Muslims to dinner, it goes without saying that pork or alcohol (even in cooking!) are not served. It is good to assure this casually in the invitation. It is a sign of respect for the other faith to be sure that the meat is from a ceremonially butchered (kosher) animal.

One can even invite Muslim friends and neighbors to dinner during the fasting month of Ramadan; one must only be sure that food (and drink!) are offered only after sunset. It is best to ask your guests the exact times to be certain.

It is a special sign of good neighborly relations if one receives a gift of meat from the sacrificial animal during the sacrificial festival (*Id-al-Adha*). One need have no concerns about accepting it. It is likewise a friendly sign if neighbors (generally only women) are invited to the *mevlit*, a memorial ceremony some Muslims observe that takes place forty days after the death or burial of a loved one. At this occasion Qur'anic verses and religious poems are recited.

Muslims consider it an honor to be greeted on Islamic holidays. Just as they might greet Christian neighbors and colleagues with "Happy Easter," for example, they regard it as a sign of respect for their own faith when one greets them before the sacrificial feast (*Id-al-Adha*) or wishes "happy holiday" for the celebration at the end of the month of fasting (*Id-al-Fitr*).

The celebration of circumcision actually is not a religious event, but a familial, societal one. The gifts that guests bring are intended to soothe the boy in his pain; gifts of money are also gladly accepted.

People invited to a Muslim wedding can treat the matter of giving a gift according to their own tradition. Often guests are invited only to the civil ceremony, while the religious ceremony is held before the imam, the leader in congregational prayer, with only close relatives and friends present.

Even if one pays attention to these initial suggestions, it is not at all assured that encounters will be successful. Too much hardening and rejection may have already taken place, and prejudices are often already stronger—on both sides—than someone with a bit of goodwill can resolve merely by attempting a fresh start. Many Muslims have a feeling that they are tolerated as guests in a society or as members on the periphery of society. Such attitudes cannot be overcome easily. We need to know that our encounters with Muslims are not to be contrived or forced, but rather prized as gifts shared between two equal partners.

It is important to understand something of the faith of Muslims so that our relationships with Muslims do not remain purely superficial. The purpose of this book is to further that understanding.

## PART ONE

# Islam—Faith and Life

HAIDERKHANA MOSQUE IN BAGHDAD

# 1

## The Qur'an

The Qur'an is the fundamental source of faith for Muslims. From this book they get their laws, as well as guidance on what to do in the various situations of life. They begin to become intimately acquainted with its content from early childhood. Non-Arab Muslims are also required to read it in its original Arabic, aloud if at all possible. By being familiar with the original Arabic of the Qur'an, all Muslims feel connected in a worldwide community.

### THE QUR'AN:
### THE WORD OF GOD

Muslims call the Qur'an the "Word of God." In this they differ from Christians, who define the "Word of God" as the Bible and above all as the "Word of God" who became flesh in Jesus Christ.

Muslims believe that the entire text of the Qur'an was revealed to Muhammad. This revelation did not occur suddenly, but spanned a period of twenty-two years, from 610 to 632, the year of Muhammad's death.

How do Muslims understand the process of this revelation? It is completed in four stages:

1. Speech (that is, God's word) is with God in heaven, eternal, like God. Sometimes this speech is metaphorically called "the Mother of the Book," that is, as the heavenly source of the Qur'an (see Sura 13.39; 43.4).
2. From this heavenly source, an angel takes those parts that are to be brought to earth at a certain point in time and shares them with God's prophet. As a rule it is the archangel Gabriel who is entrusted with this task.
3. The angel seeks out God's prophet and whispers the text word for word. The prophet is to recite this text to his people or his community, without omitting or adding words. Especially trusted followers write down the text and collect it. Thus evolves, finally, the Qur'an.
4. The book known as the Qur'an is a collection of all the revelations. Nothing in the texts may be altered by the copyists and collectors, because then the word of God would be mingled with human thoughts.

This form of revelation is not limited to Muhammad and the Qur'an according to the Muslim faith. The Qur'an also names other great prophets, especially Moses and his five books (*taurat*), David and the Psalter (*zabur*), but also Jesus and the Gospels (*injil*), which, as a unit, Muslims assume was also first recited. As Muslims see it, however, parts of these books of the earlier prophets of God, when oral tradition became written, underwent changes in the process; therefore they no longer agree with the heavenly source. For this reason God sent a prophet one more time, namely Muhammad, who would now impart the conclusive book of revelation, which is safe from further adulterations.

Muhammad heard the revelations in his Arabic mother tongue and recited them to his followers in this language. The stylistic beauty of the Qur'an's Arabic impressed his followers as well as his enemies. Non-Arabic people who later converted to Islam joined in this reverence for the Arabic text of the Qur'an. The first translations came about only tentatively; these were called *tafsir*, interpretation. They were intended to help people understand the content of the Qur'an better. Still, they could only incompletely render the vast richness of the Arabic original. For this reason the Arabic original is normally included side by side with every translation made by Muslims.

## WHAT DOES *QUR'AN* MEAN?

The word *Qur'an* in Arabic means "reading," "recitation," of a holy text. *Qur'an* originates from the verb *qura'a. Iqra* or "command to read" is the first word in the oldest revelation that Muhammad recited. According to ancient tradition, it is found in Sura 96.1-5.

Originally every revelation recited by Muhammad during a certain period was called *qur'an;* that means there were many qur'ans. These were written down and collected by some of Muhammad's followers who happened to be present. Some of them had extensive collections, others less complete. Some followers committed them to memory.

According to tradition, Muhammad received the first revelation in the year 610, following *Laylat al-Qadr,* the "night of power" (see Sura 97). This event is celebrated annually on one of the last nights of the month of fasting, Ramadan, as the "Descent of the Qur'an."

## THE QUR'AN AS A BOOK

As long as Muhammad was alive, no one saw any problem with the unsystematic manner in which the qur'ans were collected. Whenever there might be difficulties with a text, Muhammad could resolve them.

As more and more collectors and knowledgeable people died in the wars with the non-Islamic Arab tribes following Muhammad's death, Muslims became aware of the danger that one day the knowledge of the text of the revelations could also be lost. The third caliph, Uthman, in 653, twenty years after Muhammad's death, succeeded in collecting a single Qur'an text with the help of the most knowledgeable experts. This included all texts recognized as being authentic. In particular they tried to distinguish the true revelations from Muhammad's other utterances, which did not originate in the "heavenly source." Through this process, in Uthman's time, an authoritative Qur'anic text was established. This alone was to be used in performing the worship service, in making judgments in legal disputes, or in deciding theological questions.

At that time the Arabic script was not yet fully developed, however. Some letters were easily confused; moreover, vowels were not yet indicated in writing. Those wanting to read the text correctly were dependent on those who had committed it to memory. Among those there was some disagreement as to the correct pronunciation of certain texts. They also differed on the numbering of the verses. Not until 1923 did the famous Islamic University Al-Azhar in Cairo publish a thoroughly examined text, which the leaders hoped would be recognized one day by all Muslims as the sole reading text. They also attempted to fix the verse numbering.

## ON THE SEQUENCE OF THE QUR'AN

The Qur'an text is divided into chapters and verses. The chapters are called *suras*, the meaning of which is still unclear. There are a total of 114 suras. A verse is called an *ayah*, "sign," because every verse is seen as a miracle of God.

The suras are generally arranged according to length with the exception of the first sura. This sura opens the book with a prayer— thus its name, *al-Fatiha*, "The Opening." The long suras come first, with the shorter ones correspondingly farther back. Since the varying lengths of the suras were awkward for recitation, especially in Ramadan, the month of fasting, the entire text was divided again into thirty roughly equal reading portions. Each sura has a name, which generally refers to a theme or a key word.

## ON THE CONTENT OF THE QUR'AN

The Muslim finds everything in the Qur'an that is needed for a God-pleasing life in preparation for eternal life. The Qur'an contains fundamental utterances concerning:

1. faith convictions, such as faith in the oneness of God, the prophets and chosen ones, the angels, and the last judgment;
2. orders for service to God, which includes fasting during the month of Ramadan and the rites during the *hajj*, pilgrimage to Mecca;
3. societal order, particularly concerning family law; and
4. moral-ethical standards, according to which all Muslims must orient their lives.

The convictions of the faith were later studied in Islamic theology, while the Islamic legal system dealt with the other three areas. Islamic law, like Islamic theology, depends on revelation and is not a secular science.

## ON THE INTERPRETATION OF THE QUR'AN

While the Qur'an is deemed by Muslims to be of divine origin, that did not prevent difficulties arising in its interpretation. Some of these difficulties were resolved by researching into the occasions in Muhammad's life that were the settings of particular revelations. Understanding the "reasons for its descent" could clarify the meaning of a text. Still, some verses retained a "dark" or ambiguous meaning. These "dark" verses were to be interpreted by verses with a clear meaning. Furthermore, in some cases in which verses might appear to be in contradiction, the principle of abrogation was invoked, which allowed for revelation in stages. In this way, the earlier revelation or guidance was to be understood in the light of or superceded by a later revelation. Sometimes texts were interpreted with great freedom so that whenever a literal explanation led to theological difficulties, it was explained metaphorically. Thus, for example, God's sitting on a throne is not to be understood literally—because that would make God like humans—but rather as a metaphor of God's power. Others, however, usually called "fundamentalist" today, try to hold as much as possible to the literal meaning. These differing views can lead to conflict with modern understandings of justice, particularly in the area of criminal law.

# 2

# Muhammad

## FACTS OF MUHAMMAD'S LIFE

Muhammad was born in A.D. 570 on the Arabian Peninsula (now Saudi Arabia) in the oasis city of Mecca. He was a member of an impoverished family from the house of the Quraysh, who ruled Mecca at that time. He grew up as an orphan under the care of his uncle Abu Talib, whose son Ali later became one of his closest disciples. Early in life he already had to earn his keep in the service of merchants in Mecca. At twenty-five he married a wealthy widow Khadijah, for whom he had first worked as a business manager. She bore him two sons who both died in childhood and four daughters. Only through his daughter Fatimah, later the wife of Ali, did he have male descendants.

Like many pious seekers of his time, called *hanif*, Muhammad sought the knowledge of the true God in the loneliness of the desert. As the Islamic tradition reports it, in 610 the archangel Gabriel appeared to him in the cave Hira and commanded:

Proclaim! (or Read!) In the name of thy Lord and Cherisher, who created—created man, out of a (mere) clot of congealed blood:

Proclaim! And thy Lord Is Most Bountiful—He Who taught (the use of) the Pen—taught man that which he knew not. (Sura 98.1-5)

Following this Muhammad began to preach the goodness of the creator God and to warn of the imminent judgment day; he called for conversion to the one true God. In doing so he put himself in direct opposition to the Arab tribes, even to his own family, who honored various gods. Religious festivals, pilgrimages to the idols at the holy place of the Kaaba in Mecca, and the trade markets connected with these things formed an important source of income for the upper class of the city. Muhammad's call for conversion demanded integrity in trade and justice with respect to slaves, women, and orphans. The tensions between the leading merchant families and Muhammad and his followers grew in intensity. Accordingly, Muhammad advised some of his comrades to emigrate in 615 to Christian Ethiopia.

When Muhammad lost the protection of his extended family in 619 through the death of his wife and his uncle, he came into great difficulties. Because he felt increasingly threatened, he accepted an invitation three years later to move to an oasis then still known as Yathrib, where he already had a circle of followers. The year of Muhammad's emigration from Mecca to Yathrib, 622, called the Hijrah (or Hegira), begins the Islamic calendar. Yathrib was soon thereafter called Medina, *"madinat an-nabi,"* "the City of the Prophet."

Muhammad succeeded in uniting the Arab clans who were feuding over control of the city into the *umma,* the "community of God." To advance this goal, he created a community law. Three local Arab-Jewish clans were included in the negotiations. Muhammad himself took over resolution of all legal disputes. The divine instructions he was announcing gained an increasingly legal character.

The disputes with the inhabitants of Mecca continued. In 624 battle broke out at Badr, some ninety miles south of Medina. Although Muhammad and his followers had greatly inferior numbers, they were victorious. Muslims still interpret this as a miracle of God and a confirmation of Muhammad's divine calling.

In the following period, as the Islamic message spread, members of the Jewish clans in Medina and the few Christians who lived there for the most part left the area. Muhammad was convinced that he proclaimed the same faith as Jews and Christians and initially hoped they would recognize him as prophet. However, secret connections between the Jews in Medina and his opponents in Mecca, and their contention that he was falsifying the biblical message, meant the end of their protective alliance. Judged to have broken treaties, three Jewish clans were excluded from the Medinan community.

Some of the leaders of Mecca converted to Islam. In 628 the authorities of Mecca bowed to Muhammad's increasing political and religious influence and allowed him free access to the Kaaba for the month of fasting, Ramadan. When he arrived in Mecca in 630, accompanied by his troops, the residents of Mecca yielded without much resistance. He cleansed the Kaaba of its idols. Following this triumph it became increasingly clear that the message entrusted to Muhammad was not just for Arabs but was the true religion for all humanity.

Muhammad thought that belief in the oneness of God was endangered among Christians because they honored Jesus as the Son of God. To signify a clear differentiation from Judaism and Christianity, the direction of prayer was changed: Muslims no longer turned toward Jerusalem like the Jews, but rather toward Mecca. Thus Mecca became the center of Islam (see Sura 2.142-150). Muhammad proclaimed that Abraham had erected the first "House of God," the Kaaba in Mecca, as a place to honor the one God.

Muhammad generously forgave his opponents and by doing so won many new followers among his former enemies. Then he returned to his family in Medina. He made his first and only formal pilgrimage to the holy Kaaba in Mecca in 632. Muslims making the pilgrimage today still follow the ritual to which he submitted himself.

In the years following the death of his first wife Khadijah, Muhammad married twelve women; among them were a number of widows who were left without means because their Muslim husbands had died in battle, though one was a Christian and one a Jew. He justified the unusually high number by means of special divine permission. Muslims see these marriages as his show of compassion for widows who otherwise had no means of support. Muhammad died without a male heir on June 8, 632, in the home of his favorite wife, Aisha; he had not chosen a successor for the leadership of the *umma*. He was buried in Medina.

Muhammad was a prophet as well as a politician. In Mecca he appeared as a preacher of judgment and messenger of a renewed faith. The Islamic state he founded is still the model in Islam today.

## "THE SEAL OF THE PROPHETS"

The Qur'an teaches that Muhammad was a servant of God, without any superhuman powers, exceptional only in the special duty to be God's prophet and messenger:

> Say thou: "I am but a man like you: It is revealed to me by inspiration, that your God is One God." (Sura 41.6)

and:

> Say: "I tell you not that with me are the treasures of Allah, nor do I know what is hidden, nor do I tell you I am an angel. I but follow what is revealed to me."
> Say: "Can the blind be held equal to the seeing? Will ye then consider not?" (Sura 6.50)

Thus Muhammad indicates that it was by a miracle that the ability to communicate the Qur'an was given to him, an uneducated person.

Other proclamations of the Qur'an describe Muhammad as a model for the faithful. The numerous model stories from Muhammad's life demonstrate this. Muslims are bound to abide by these *hadith*, "traditions."

Soon the life and sayings of Muhammad were surrounded with particular reverence and had a strong influence on the piety of Muslims. The profound reverence for everything that had to do with the life of their prophet and the reports that his contemporaries gave of him led to numerous legends, poems, and songs of praise for the prophet. From early on just saying his name was believed to have a blessed effect. Recently Muhammad's birthday has been gaining importance as a special day, though some object to this on the grounds that remembering it makes too much of a mortal.

Islam has always maintained that Muhammad was only human, and that the encounter between God and humanity is only completed in the process of revelation, not in a person; thus Muslims do not want to be called "Muhammadans." In spite of these objections, Muhammad gained superhuman qualities in the common people's piety; they saw him as the perfect Muslim. Mysterious events were reported from his life. It is said, for instance, that his breast had been opened in his childhood and his heart purified so that he would be able to receive the divine revelation unstained. Especially important is the story of his ascension to heaven and its many-faceted history of interpretation (Sura 17.1). Muhammad had been carried off to Jerusalem on his heavenly steed (*buraq*); from there he ascended through seven heavens into paradise to see the splendor of God. On his ascent he encountered all the prophets who went before him. However, some of these stories do not belong to the Islamic articles of faith and are not found in the Qur'an.

Muhammad saw himself as one in a long line of prophets who were called by God to awaken and renew the people in their confession of the one God. God's renewed revelation to Muhammad was necessary because, in Islamic perspective, the message of the earlier prophets had been altered and falsified. By contrast with these earlier altered revelations, as in Judaism and Christianity, with the Qur'an there was but one text—"In it is guidance sure, without doubt, to those who fear Allah" (Sura 2.2).

The Qur'an expresses the universal and conclusive significance of Muhammad's mission through the image of Muhammad as "the Seal of the Prophets" (Sura 33.40). Beyond this, Muslims in conversation with Christians often refer to a Qur'an verse (Sura

61.6), according to which Jesus is supposed to have announced the coming of one more messenger of God.


## MUHAMMAD IN CHRISTIAN PERSPECTIVE

For centuries Christians have had a distorted view of Muhammad. It is time to tear down prejudices and to take account of the historical truth. Even without seeing Muhammad with the eyes of a Muslim, Christians should recognize and appreciate his great historical importance.

For Islam Muhammad is the "prophet and chosen one of God." The biblical prophets, each in a specific situation, called their people back to obedience and faith in God. Muhammad, too, as a preacher of repentance, called the people in his region to faith in the one God. This message of the holy and just God includes a considerable portion of biblical prophetic proclamation and must be taken seriously by Christians as well.

But Islam also sees Muhammad as the religious and political leader of the *umma*, the community of God. He gave to the human community an eternally valid order in the revealed Qur'an. Thus Muhammad has a similarly comprehensive meaning for Islam as Moses had for his people, as told in the Old Testament. This unity of religious and political leadership is foreign to Christians, who do not see Jesus in this way. Moreover, Christians cannot recognize the Islamic claim that Muhammad brings the conclusive, universally valid revelation by which even the gospel of Jesus Christ would have to be measured. In contrast, Christians confess that God's truth and salvation appeared once for all time in the person of Jesus Christ, as the Bible testifies. It is distressing to Muslims that Christians cannot see the prophet Muhammad as Muslims do; and it distresses Christians that their confession of Jesus Christ does not strengthen their relationship with Muslims, but rather separates them. Thus conversation about Muhammad—and about Jesus Christ—is a mutual responsibility for Christians and Muslims.

# 3

# The Five Pillars of Islam
# The First Two:
# Testimony and Prayer

Islam is built on "five pillars" for living, five religious duties, as the foundation for submission to God:

- the declaration of faith in the confession, *shahadah*.
- the performance of traditional prayer, *salat*, five times daily. The prayer, like the confession, is spoken in Arabic.
- gifts of alms to the poor, *zakat*. This follows clearly specified rates and puts into practice social responsibility for one another.
- the practice of self-control and discipline through fasting, *sawm*, during the entire month of Ramadan.
- the pilgrimage to Mecca, *hajj*. This should be made once in a lifetime if at all possible, but only if the family does not incur a financial crisis as a result.

This chapter will look at the first two pillars; chapter 4 will review the other three.

## TESTIMONY TO THE ONE GOD

> There is no God but Allah (*la ilaha illa-Llah* [Allah]) and Muhammad is his prophet (*wa anna Muhammad rasulu Llah* [Allah]).

These are the basic creeds of Islam. Sura 112 expands on the first statement:

> Say: He is Allah, the One and Only; Allah, the Eternal, Absolute; He begetteth not, nor is He begotten; and there is none like unto Him.

With these words Islam puts itself in irreconcilable opposition to all faiths that believe in many gods, and as we will see, to Christianity, which holds that Jesus is the Son of God.

At the same time its closeness to Judaism and Christianity becomes clear: In Islam, too, the primary concern is for the right relationship of humanity with the one and only God. When Muslims call God Allah, they use the Arabic word *ilah*, which originally referred to the highest god from pre-Islamic times. This word is related to the Hebrew terms for God, *eloah* and *elohim*. Allah literally means "the God." Arab Christians also use the term Allah for God.

Muhammad viewed himself as a member of the long line of prophets who warn people of God's judgment and call them to repentance and a responsible life. This line began with Adam and Noah, and continued with Abraham, Moses, David, and Jesus, up to Muhammad. Abraham became a paradigm of faith for all time through his obedience to God and his upright way of living. For this reason the Qur'an calls people to follow the "way of Abraham" (Sura 4:125). Moses and Jesus, according to the Qur'an, had the task of purifying this faith from errors and distortions. Muhammad was convinced that he was not bringing anything new, but that it rather was a revelation in agreement with all the prophets before him. In his view Christians had strayed from faith in the one God through their confession of Jesus as God's Son and of the Trinity. Here we again see a division between Islam and Christianity.

Islam does recognize Jews and Christians as "people of the book" who base their lives respectively on the law of Moses and the Torah, or on the message of Jesus, the gospel. But the Qur'an at the same time calls them to:

> Say: "O People of the Book! come to common terms as between us and you: that we worship none but Allah; that we associate no partners with Him." (Sura 3.64)

In the view of Muslims, the Qur'an contains everything in perfect form that was present in the earlier revelations but has been partially falsified.

## THE POSITION OF HUMANITY BEFORE GOD

God, the One, expects humans to recognize the divine greatness and majesty, and to submit and obey. This is the heart of Islam, complete submission. Islam means "self-surrender" and "service." The promise is given that through this submission people will both find their appropriate place and achieve peace (*salam*, compare to the Hebrew *shalom*). People become *abd Allah*, laborers and servants of God, and thus have their human worth. They are obligated to be available for the service of their Lord, and to put the entire earth under God's lordship.

Although humanity is subordinate to God, as is appropriate, humanity is at the same time elevated above all creation. God's word reveals in the Qur'an that humans are placed as the vice-regents (*khalifah*, compare to *caliph*) over the earth and over all creation (Sura 2.30).

In the Qur'an God gave the correct understanding of the kind of order intended for the world that would sustain life. This gave guidance for humans so that they might live according to this divine will. This is God's mercy, that he revealed this "right guidance." Thereby people become responsible for their lives and accountable to God for all their deeds and omissions. Islam, too, as well as

Judaism and Christianity, awaits the resurrection of the dead at the last judgment. Faith and obedience are to determine how to live in all circumstances. That is why it is the greatest sin for people to depend on something other than God: doing so rejects God's sole leadership. They put something beside God, which they see as an additional source of power. This is the unforgivable sin of *shirk*, "association with other deities or partners": People should trust only in God. "God is greater than everything"—*Allahu akbar*, according to the briefest form of confession.

## THE TRADITIONS

Muslims depend on many resources in order to mold their lives in an upright manner before God. Besides the Qur'an, they have reports of the prophet Muhammad's example and his decisions in many questions about life in the first community, as well as stories about the exemplary activities of the prophet's disciples. These reports and stories demonstrate how the foundational rules of the Qur'an are to be applied. They serve as the binding tradition (*sunna*) and as a second source for the correct teaching and behavior of Muslims. These teaching stories (*hadith*) were originally passed on orally.

Their content has been organized and codified in the *sharia*: laws and rules for Islamic life that often go into the minutest detail. Developments during the first centuries of the Islamic community and its faith and life also contributed to shaping the sharia.

## THE SECOND PILLAR:
## SELF-SURENDER IN PRAYER

Muslims' daily routine achieves a regular pattern through traditional prayer five times daily: before sunrise, at noon, in the afternoon, at sundown, and before sleeping. Events of the day are continually interrupted by prayer, and people are reminded that they must lead their lives and be responsible before God. If Muslims cannot carry out a prayer at the specified time, they can make it up later.

The inner submission is expressed in the gestures of the ritual prayer. When praying in the direction of the Kaaba in Mecca, the faithful are reminded of the unity of all Muslims and the central place for worship.

At the same time the external forms of prayer and the words used connect all Muslims of all times and places; for they originated in Muhammad's practice of prayer and are carried out in the same manner everywhere.

The community is emphasized even more prominently in the Friday prayer, to which all are obligated. In long, close rows they kneel prostrate behind the prayer leaders.

## THE ORDER OF PRAYER

*Niyah,* "intention to pray": The persons praying first declare that they pray to God alone. Then they begin to purify themselves. Carefully Muslims wash their hands, mouths, noses, faces, underarms, ears, necks, and feet. Purified and inwardly prepared, they enter the prayer room of the mosque.

*Qiyam,* "the standing": Muslims begin their actual prayer standing, looking in the direction of Mecca. They remember the perfection and greatness of God and take refuge in him from the hated Evil One. After this they pray the first sura, *al-Fatiha.* This represents the summation and heart of the holy book and the most beautiful prayer of Islam:

> . . . Show us the straight way, the way of those on whom Thou hast bestowed Thy Grace, those whose (portion) is not wrath, and who go not astray. (Sura 1.6-7)

This sura is often followed by another (often Sura 112).

*Ruku,* "kneeling": With the words *Allahu akbar,* those praying bow in order to pay homage to God in humility: "Praise be to my great Lord."

In rising they respond: "O God, all praise to you."

The persons praying repeat the bowing with the same words in order to reaffirm that they are prepared to subordinate themselves to God completely.

*Sujud,* "falling prostrate," the middle of the prayer: Those praying kneel and twice bend forward until they touch the ground with their foreheads. At the same time they repeat the confession formula, *Allahu akbar.* Thus submission to God takes place, giving God the honor: "Honor be with my most high Lord." Here, too, the earnestness of the action is underscored by repetition.

Muslims witness from this center of their prayer: "Here we feel very close to God. Here he surrounds us; here we find peace— *salam.*"

The course of obligatory prayer requires this cycle at least once five times a day: before sunrise, at noon, in the afternoon, at sundown, and before sleep.

*At-tashahhud,* "the recitation": While sitting from a kneeling position, the confession of faith is recited, followed by the petition for blessing that God gave the ancient father Abraham. The faithful use some of the words Abraham himself is supposed to have said: "Our Lord, forgive us on the day of judgment for our debt, and be gracious with me, my parents, and all who believe."

*Taslim,* "greeting of peace": The greeting of peace follows this petition. The faithful turn to the right and the left and thus greet all present as well as all who are praying in the direction of Mecca from other places: "*As-salamu alaykum wa rahmatu-Llah*"—"Peace be with you and God's mercy!"

When Muslims have completed this traditional part of prayer, they keep sitting and say further prayers from the tradition. For this meditative portion, they often use prayer beads. They repeat (thirty-three times each) the central statements of Islam: "Praise be to God!" "Every thanks is due to God!" "God is greater!" or they contemplate the characteristics of God by naming the "ninety-nine most beautiful names for God," while the beads slide through their fingers. Then they can freely formulate requests and prayers, called *dua*. *Du'a* is permitted in the people's native languages.

In the starkly pronounced communal character of Islamic prayer, it is clear that each person praying is accepted as a brother or sister in the "House of Islam." In Islam there is only one distinction between people that counts: On one side are those who submit to God—this is the meaning of the word *Muslim*—and on the other are those who deny God.

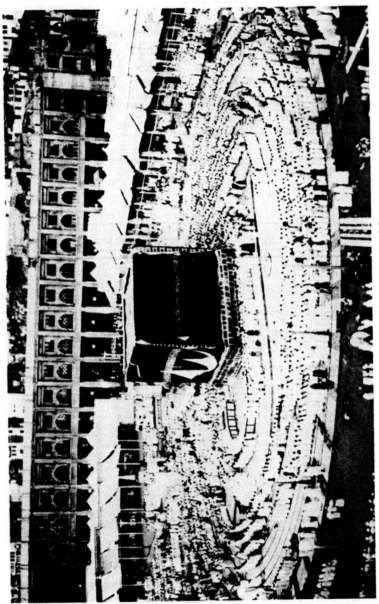

THE KAABA, THE HOLY SHRINE IN MECCA

# 4

## The Five Pillars of Islam
## The Next Three:
## Fasting, Almsgiving,
## and Pilgrimage

### THE THIRD PILLAR: FASTING *(SAWM)*

For Muslims, the third pillar of Islam, the daytime fast during the month of Ramadan, is the most important sign of religious faithfulness aside from daily prayer. Muslims tell of a tradition from the time of their prophet: Whoever fasts through the month of Ramadan with faith and a sense of responsibility will be forgiven for past sins by God. A duty fulfilled in the month of Ramadan is worth seventy duties fulfilled in other months. Ramadan is the month of patience, and the reward for patience is paradise. Ramadan is the month of reconciliation; it is the month whose beginning is mercy, whose middle is forgiveness, and whose end is freedom from the fire of hell.

Ramadan imposes a severe discipline on Muslims. From the first appearance of the new month, each morning the faithful affirm their intention to fast on this day. From that moment on, when at dawn a black and a white thread can be distinguished, they do not eat, drink, smoke, or engage in sexual intercourse until sundown.

This discipline lasts for a full four weeks until the crescent of the new moon of the following month becomes visible.

Muslims commemorate the night of the twenty-seventh day of Ramadan as the night that Muhammad first heard the Qur'anic message (*Laylat al-Qadr*, "Night of Power" or "Night of Destiny"). It is thus a holy night in Islam; for on this night the angel and the spirit descended with permission of the Lord. It is a night full of blessing (see Sura 44.1-8).

Many Muslims read the entire Qur'an in the month of Ramadan; Qur'an recitations and instruction take place in all mosques. The faithful refer back to the example of Muhammad himself. The story says that the archangel Gabriel came to him during Ramadan in Medina night after night to recite and meditate on the Qur'an with him. Thus this month becomes a time for renewed self-dedication to God: many people decide to turn back from their mistaken ways, to let themselves be guided aright in the community by the Qur'an.

Through the discipline of the fast that Muslims experience, they honor God as well as demonstrate that they belong to a large community. For this reason many feel shut out from the community when they cannot fast due to illness or old age, even though they are expressly excused from the duty to fast in these circumstances. Young people feel a sense of pride and the community celebrates when for the first time they take the fast upon themselves. It is intended that this should lead to discipline of one's entire life: a discipline of the tongue, so that it does not lie or slander; of the ears, so that they will shut out evil; and of all desire, so that it is directed toward God's will. At the same time the month of fasting is a period of reconciliation among people and a time for helping the poor in their midst. This is all made visible during the three-day celebration of breaking the fast. This celebration, *Id-al-Fitr*, "The feast of breaking fast," is celebrated with great joy by the whole community. At the beginning a public worship service is held, attended primarily by men. The mosque is usually much too small for it. Following this service, people visit one another and exchange gifts.

Because the Islamic year strictly follows the lunar year, which is shorter than the solar year, Ramadan falls eleven days earlier each year than the previous year.

## THE FOURTH PILLAR: GIVING OF ALMS (ZAKAT)

Chronologically early suras of the Qur'an already warn:

> Seest thou one who denies the Judgment (to come)? Then such is the (man) who repulses the orphan (with harshness), and encourages not the feeding of the indigent. So woe to the worshippers who . . . refuse (to supply) (even) neighborly needs. (Sura 107)

The Qur'an also early commends generosity:

> Those who remain steadfast to their prayer; and those in whose wealth is a recognised right for the (needy) who asks and him who is prevented (for some reason from asking). (Sura 70.23-25)

> Those who spend their wealth for increase in self-purification . . . to seek for the Countenance of their Lord Most High. (Sura 92.18, 20)

Islam, however, wants to get beyond mere spontaneous help at times of emergency (*sadaqah*). After the emigration of Muhammad and his friends from Mecca to Medina, some were in such dire straits that new rules had to be created. These new rules were deemed permanently valid: Whoever had possessions was obligated to give a contribution. This was seen as a demand by God for the sake of equity (Sura 2.110).

Sura 9.60 states that these donations will be used:

- for the poor and needy;
- for officials appointed over them (such as social service workers);
- for poor people who could be won over to Islam or who, when converting to Islam, were in danger of loss of life or poverty;

- for people in the "cause of Allah," who serve by teaching the faith and so spread it or defend it, and for this reason have no other income; and
- for travelers in need.

The rule is that all adult, healthy Muslims are to give 2.5 percent annually of their property and earnings from crafts, industry, or business or 10 percent of earnings from their harvest of crops or ownership of livestock. The poor are free of this obligation.

With the close unity of state and religion in Muslim society, it has not always been possible to distinguish between charity and taxes. Still the *zakat* (gifts of alms) has always remained a vital moral obligation in private life. The amazingly high contributions that Muslims in Europe or North America send to their home countries, primarily at the end of Ramadan, and their donations for mosques in the country where they now live are impressive demonstrations of *zakat*.

The attitude that lies behind the law of charitable contributions is taken very seriously in modern reform movements. One is obligated to use all one's earnings and income for the help of society. In a community truly characterized by Islam, no unjust conditions ought to exist. In the years past, many Muslims hoped to find in Islam a third choice beyond Western capitalism and Eastern communism. They saw both approaches as contradicting the brotherhood of humanity before God. In both cases each person had wealth at the expense of others, which is regarded as "stolen goods," *haram* (literally "forbidden"). People who strive for inflated earnings or demand high interest rates are also condemned (*riba*, Sura 2.275-281). Islamic society should refuse the charging of interest (Sura 3.130). For this reason Islamic banks try to find new ways for investment by "risk sharing" or "profit sharing."


## THE FIFTH PILLAR: THE PILGRIMAGE
## TO MECCA (*HAJJ*)

Some two months after Ramadan begins, the pilgrimage to Mecca commences. These are days of great religious importance not only for the pilgrims, but for all Muslims. They are reminded that they belong to the *umma*, the worldwide community of Islam, which binds people together beyond class and ethnic diversity through faith in the one God.

Pilgrims from all parts of the world converge on Mecca. In recent years this has amounted to far more than 1.5 million people annually. While still near the Red Sea coast, all exchange their regular, ethnic clothes for the same simple white garments: two seamless cloths for men, a loose ankle-length dress for women, and, at the most, sandals on their feet. This is to emphasize the equality of all people before God, whatever their race or nation or social standing.

As soon as the pilgrims cross the borders of the city of Mecca, they begin calling *Labbayka-Llahumma labbayk*, "At thy service, my God, at thy service." During the seven days of pilgrimage they continually dedicate themselves with this confession.

The pilgrimage goes back to an express command in the Qur'an (Sura 22.27). Muhammad himself ordered the details in 632, shortly before his death. In it he saw the completion of his task, and he promised pilgrims paradise as a reward for their journey. He demanded that everyone who completed the pilgrimage should be treated with the utmost respect.

The first of the rites in Mecca is circling the Kaaba seven times. The Kaaba is a cube-shaped building about twelve by twelve yards in area in the courtyard of the great mosque in Mecca and completely covered with a black cloth. While performing this rite the pilgrims kiss the black stone set in silver that is built into a corner of the Kaaba wall. It is probably a meteorite. According to Muslim tradition Abraham received this stone from the archangel Gabriel when he received his assignment, together with his son Ishmael, to build this "place of prayer" (Sura 2.124-127).

Mecca's significance according to Arab legend goes back to Adam. There, following his expulsion from the garden and after a long search, the first man found Eve, the mother of all humanity.

Thus Mecca for Muslims is the place where God was close to people in mercy from the beginning, and "the mother of cities" was the center of all human habitation. That is why they turn toward it in prayer and also often hang pictures of the Kaaba or the great mosque in their homes.

The details of the pigrimage continuously refer back to Abraham and thus underscore Islam's claim to be the best religion for all humanity:

1. The pilgrims circle the Kaaba. This encircling is followed by the traditional prayer at "the station of Abraham," where it is believed he performed his devotions.
2. The pilgrims then run seven times between the hills Safa and Marwa that are located near the great mosque. At this time the story is told of Hagar, Abraham's second wife, and how she desperately sought water for her son Ishmael. This ritual is repeated at the end of the pilgrimage when the pilgrims drink from the Zamzam well.
3. On the fourth day a sermon is preached in the great mosque. As with all the rituals of the pilgrimage, its message is to seal anew the submission of people before God.
4. On the fifth day the pilgrims go to Arafat to spend an entire day in prayer. This is the day for making a new vow of submission to God, as well as one of breaking with old vices (such as smoking or drinking) and one of help for the faithful poor so that they also may fulfill the pilgrimage, the *hajj*.
5. On the seventh day, on returning from the Arafat field, about 9.3 miles from Mecca, the pilgrims throw stones at the three pillars by Mina. This recalls how Abraham fended off the temptations of the devil.
6. The sacrifice of animals on the seventh day, the concluding day of pilgrimage, is performed in remembrance of Abraham and/or as a charity. The meat goes to needy people as commanded.

This is the great celebration, the sacrificial feast, *Id-al-Adha*. This recalls how God rescued Abraham's son from being sacrificed. It also shows that the right relationship of people to God is one that demands no sacrifice, and certainly no human sacrifice. What is demanded, rather, is submission to God by obedience to God's will, as the Qur'an and the sunna of the prophet demonstrate.

At the same time, sacrificial animals are slaughtered ritually all over the world. On this day Muslims everywhere feel connected with the pilgrims in Mecca in a special way as well as with all the faithful throughout the world.

The pilgrimage is prescribed in the same manner for women and men. It is an obligation for all once in their lifetime if they can complete it without bringing their family into financial need and suffering. If people cannot come at the time of the great pilgrimage to Mecca, then they should at least make the lesser pilgrimage, called *umra*, at another time of year.

# 5

## Justice and Law

God gave humanity the law in order to give humanity right guidance. *Sharia,* the Arabic word for the religious law in Islam, originally meant "the way that leads to the oasis." Whoever follows God's sharia does not die in the desert but finds the water of life. Devout Muslims therefore strive to know God's laws in order to do good and avoid evil, and so remain in the "right guidance" of God. According to Islamic understanding such people are well off—like the pious one of the Old Testament who is praised in the first psalm (Ps. 1:1-3):

> Happy are those
> who do not follow the advice of the wicked,
> or take the path that sinners tread,
>     or sit in the seat of scoffers;
> but their delight is in the law of the LORD,
>     and on his law they meditate day and night.
> They are like trees
>     planted by streams of water,
> which yield their fruit in its season,

and their leaves do not wither.
In all that they do, they prosper.

Such an attitude brings people's actions into the foreground
of religious interest, where they are directed and measured by the
commandments and prohibitions of divine law. Thus Muslims, too,
are happy when people follow the law and order given by God.

## THE LAW—GOD'S GOOD GIFT

The word *Islam* means submission to God, subjection to God's will.
God intended people to be his "vice-regents" or caliphs (Sura 2.30).
By doing this he did not just give them power to use the earth,
but the responsibility as well to protect its order in accordance with
creation. So too they must learn to bring their lives and actions
into harmony with God's law, for their own salvation, for the benefit
of all creation, and for God's glory.

Yet people do not do justice to this provision. That is why
God in his mercy has continually sent prophets. They have taught
God's law and brought the light of "right guidance." Justice and
law for Muslims are not just burdensome boundaries or a trouble-
some task, but proof of God's mercy; God shows his creatures the
right way.

The eternal divine law was proclaimed by the prophets among
different peoples and communities with particular historical expressions. However, Muhammad received God's law conclusively,
and it is binding for all people. For Muslims it is an ideal that
incorporates all aspects of life's experience: the confession of faith;
traditional laws and service to God; ethical foundations for the
individual, the family, the community; provisions for family, criminal, and sociopolitical law.

## THE SHAPING OF ISLAMIC LAW

During its first centuries Islam worked intensively at realizing this
ideal in the Islamic community. For this purpose principles for

determining justice were set up and rules for their application developed. Thus the system of Islamic jurisprudence (*fiqh*) arose, carried on by the scholars (*ulama*), who were both lawyers and theologians.

## Qur'an

The first source and most important foundation of Islamic law is the Qur'an itself. It contains long legal stipulations, particularly in the later parts that date from the Medina period. At this time the Islamic commonwealth was formed in Medina under Muhammad's leadership and the Qur'anic instructions formed the decisive guiding principles.

## Sunna

With the expansion of the Islamic empire and with the passage of time after Muhammad had died, new questions arose regarding the practice of law. To answer these, Islamic authorities were compelled in the absence of clear direction to refer to conventional laws of the existing order, as well as to some of non-Islamic origin. Nevertheless, the lawyers tried as best they could to orient themselves to the Qur'an and the life experiences of Muhammad and his disciples as told in the sunna. These traditions remained alive in many stories and formulations, though genuine and false tradition were mixed together. Scholars saw the need and attempted to secure the authentic form by defining a line of authorities leading back to the tradition in question and by collecting and examining the writings that had proliferated and in which they were contained. This process was concluded in the ninth century. The "Sunna of the Prophet" established at that time became the second binding source for Islamic law.

## Ijtihad

As the Prophet sent his messenger, Muadh, to Yemen, as one tradition has it, he said to him: "How will you decide?" Muadh

said: "I will decide according to what is written in God's book."
Muhammad said: "But if it does not appear in God's book?" Muadh
replied: "Then according to the way [sunna] of God's prophet."
Muhammad said: "But if it does not appear in the way of God's
prophet?" Muadh answered: "Then I will form my own judgment."
Muhammad said: "Praise be to God, who has granted success to
the messenger of God's Prophet."

This story shows that a third norm for determining justice,
supplementing the Qur'an and sunna, was sometimes needed.
*Ijtihad*, intellectual "effort," seeks to formulate a new decision or
behavior on the basis of a rational interpretation of the binding
sources of law (Qur'an and sunna). A method for doing this gained
widespread authority. In this case a judgment is made in ques-
tionable situations on the basis of an analogy (*qiyas*) with cases that
were clear and had already been dealt with in the Qur'an and sunna.

### Ijma

An axiom ascribed to Muhammad states that the community of the
faithful cannot agree to an error. The fourth norm of justice derives
from this axiom: *ijma*, "the consensus of the community." This
principle was later applied to the consensus of scholars in any
given period.

The four norms of the *sharia*, the law of Islam, were developed
in the course of a long period, during which various regional
"schools of law" (*madhhab*) were developed. The lawyer Muhammad ibn Idris ash-Shafi took the decisive step at the beginning of
the ninth century: He "locked the gate of *ijtihad*," of rational judgment. This meant that new rational judgments were not allowed,
for interpretation was limited strictly to the already existing written
traditions of Qur'an and sunna. The content of the sharia and the
rules of its application became fixed.

### THE FOUR SUNNI SCHOOLS OF LAW

Sunni Islam is the orthodox tradition, and 85 percent of the world's
Muslims are Sunni. Within Sunni Islam, four schools of law have

prevailed; each relies on an authority from the classical period: the successors of Malik ibn Anas (Malikites), Abu Hanifa (Hanafites), Muhammad ash-Shafi (Shafi'ites), and Ahmad ibn Hanbal (Hanbalites). The differences between them are less in content than in their methods of determining justice. For example, the Hanafite school, which most Turks follow, still allows relative freedom to use reasonable judgment. On the other hand, the Hanbalite school, followed in Saudi Arabia, holds to the traditional principle strictly. Actually, the people in all Islamic countries can follow any of the schools of law, but belonging to one of them is an important element in the self-perception of all Muslims. Shi'ite Islam developed its own law tradition.

Islamic law is formulated as a religious doctrine of duty. It orders all human activities and relations in five categories: "commanded" (*fard*) and "forbidden" (*haram*); "recommended" (*mustahabb*) and "discouraged" (*mahruh*); as well as the neutral "permitted" (*mubah*). Still, the prescriptions of the sharia have never been unambiguously codified into one collection of laws. Marriage and family law, estate law, and religious ritual are the areas handled with the greatest degree of thoroughness in the Qur'an and sunna. They still form the core of the sharia. Other areas, especially the state, administration, tax law, and even criminal law, have been more strongly subjected to societal and political changes. They became increasingly removed from the strict control of Islamic tradition. The Ottoman empire (Turkey and surroundings) introduced a special order of law (*kanun*) alongside but distinct from the sharia to cover these areas.

## ISLAMIC LAW IN THE CONTEMPORARY WORLD

In nearly all Islamic countries today there is a combination of traditional elements with Western conceptions of law. The force of the sharia has been considerably reduced, even in those countries where it is the primary source (or one of the primary sources) for

the law according to the constitution. In modern Turkey, for example, and in other Islamic countries, the government strove to
create a secular state in an effort to modernize and compete with
European states. Thus the sharia has even been abandoned by some
as the foundation for state law. Among the population, however,
traditional norms and rules have been kept alive, especially in
matters of marriage and family law, so that a tension arises between
the law validated by the state and what is actually practiced
and lived.

In the meantime, following a general resurgence of the power
of Islam, a countermovement has set in. The sharia is again gaining
importance in the consciousness of many Muslims and in the legal
systems of individual Islamic countries. Some groups, especially
those called "fundamentalists," energetically promote the conviction that the entire life of Muslims and the society as a whole within
a state must be ordered, as it was supposed to have been in the
original Islamic community, according to God's "right guidance"
and the prescriptions of the sharia. This has led to intensive intellectual and political effort, but also to vehement arguments, within the Islamic world.

This development is made especially clear in Islamic criminal
law. The Qur'an does not contain a complete teaching on criminal
law, but only single answers to individual questions. Only five
crimes are named in the Qur'an with precisely prescribed conditions
and punishments: unchastity, slander regarding supposed unchastity, consuming any hard liquor or drugs except for medicinal
purposes, larceny, and highway robbery. The punishments serve
primarily as a warning to others. They range from death for willful
murder to stoning for unchastity, or cutting off a hand for larceny.

The Qur'an, however, limits its strict threats of punishment.
Thus the Qur'an exhorts the faithful to forgive the repentant of-
fender (Sura 5.39). Besides this the evidence of the crime must meet
unusually high standards according to the Qur'an's stipulations—
unchastity must be confirmed by four witnesses who are in agreement. In addition, the judges have considerable room for judgment
in sentencing. The rule of the *siyasa shari'iyyah* plays an important
role. *Siyasa* means "administration," and in this case refers to the

right of the state to administer the sharia flexibly in accordance with the public interest as long as the general principles of Islamic law are not violated. This flexible practice can accommodate new developments, and is based on whether crimes bring about unusual harm to the community. If they do, the punishments are more severe.

## ISLAMIC MINORITIES IN EUROPE AND NORTH AMERICA

The sharia not only includes religious laws that individual Muslims must fulfill in their private lives; it aims at public implementation throughout all of society. The sharia can be practiced fully only in a country whose internal affairs are determined by Islam. Muslim families and groups living in Europe and North America today are painfully aware of this fact. Whether it be a matter of the traditional laws of prayer or eating, or the order in marriage and family, they continuously encounter the reality that they are a minority in a non-Islamic, highly secularized environment.

Among Muslims in this situation who seek direction from the Islamic tradition, three primary approaches are taken. (1) Many Muslims want to refer back to the legal and societal status that Islam developed for the religious minorities of Jews and Christians and to renew this for themselves. This approach allows a certain self-sufficiency, especially for traditional and legal questions in the family, although it also includes the danger of ghettoization. (2) Others advocate that in a non-Islamic country the sharia has only limited validity. This position is in accordance with certain Islamic understandings of law, for example of *mustamin*, "a protected one." That is to say, those of a minority faith are given a certain protection. (3) Some follow the use of *ijtihad*, which does not question the validity of the Qur'an and sunna, but does allow a new interpretation of a problem when it is not addressed in the Qur'an or sunna. This approach thus permits an appropriate contemporary development in the application of Islamic law.

A Muslim woman at prayer

# 6

## Woman and Family

For Muslims the family is the core of the human community. God himself has given it this central importance in the societal and religious order.

### QUR'AN AND SUNNA

According to the Qur'an, men and women have the same rank before God and are created with the same worth and the same rights. Both can achieve paradise (Sura 9.72). Still God created them differently and thus gave them differing rights and responsibilities.

To Islam the idea that sexuality as such is sinful is foreign; sexuality belongs to God's good gifts and is to be realized in marriage. In the creation of woman God's grace is visible: She was created as a mate for man. The marriage partners are intended to be bound to one another in love and mercy (Sura 30.21). The woman is for the man and the man for the woman like "garments" (Sura 2.187). This means that man and woman are to give each other

**59**

warmth, protection, comfort, and joy. In his last sermon Muhammad said to his disciples: "You have a claim on your wives, and your wives have a claim on you."

The Qur'an dramatically improved the position of the woman in the family and society by securing her rights. These include a right to personal property (hardly heard of before), the right to inheritance, and comprehensive legal protection. Every woman has the right to be provided for. The married woman has a right to be supported by her husband in a style that accords with her class. At the wedding the woman has the right to a marriage contract, which stipulates the dowry and the separation fee in case of divorce, according to Sura 4.4. For her part, the woman is obligated to be a good wife to her husband and to be responsible with his property.

The husband is obligated to protect and provide for his family. According to the Qur'an he can marry as many as four wives:

> If ye fear that ye shall not be able to deal justly with the orphans, marry women of your choice, two, or three, or four; but if ye fear that ye shall not be able to deal justly (with them), then only one. (Sura 4.3)

Many interpreters see this promotion of just, equal treatment as a tendency toward endorsement of monogamy. The Qur'an says that if one cannot be just, then marry only one wife.

The husband is given a right to show dissatisfaction with his wife:

> Therefore the righteous women are devoutly obedient, and guard in (the husband's) absence what Allah would have them guard. As to those women on whose part ye fear disloyalty and ill-conduct, admonish them (first), (next), refuse to share their beds, (and last) beat them (lightly). (Sura 4.34)

These statements are interpreted and handled variously in the Islamic world. Some refer to the fact that Muhammad himself never used the right to punish.

Children are a blessing from God. Their upbringing, including religious education, belongs to the common tasks of husbands and wives. The wife has a special role; according to one of Muhammad's pronouncements, paradise lies at the feet of the mothers.

Parents and children are responsible for one another. Siblings are responsible for one another as well. According to Muhammad the older siblings have rights with regard to the younger ones analogous to those of the father over his children. The Qur'an emphasizes the obligation to care for aging parents (Sura 17.23-24).

## TRADITIONAL NEAR EASTERN SOCIETY

Life in marriage and family, and thus the position of the woman, are generally determined by the patriarchal order and the assignment of set roles in the family. Upon marriage the woman becomes a member of her husband's family. In traditional Near Eastern society the secondary role of the woman has been reemphasized. In the process, patriarchal order became the interpretive key to the Qur'an. Here are two examples:

- According to Sura 2.282, in some cases the testimony of two women before a judge is as valid as that of one man. From this the idea developed, held by some, that in public life women have only half the importance of men.
- The widespread customs of veiling the face and wearing a head covering make a similar point. Qur'anic texts that were used later as evidence for this requirement (Sura 24.31; 33.59) stipulate only that women dress decently and honorably in order to protect themselves from molestation. Actually, the Qur'an has references to dress codes for both men and women.

Some Muslims in early Islam had commandments and prohibitions for both genders, but the strict rules for boys are often neglected. In practice the prescriptions for girls and women are still remembered. Cultural customs vary among Muslims, but some especially valued are virginity in girls and restraint in women. From this follows the strict separation of genders in many Islamic societies, and the wife's restriction to the life of her family, and, when strangers visit, to private rooms. Some customs decree that a man should never meet with a woman to whom he is not married or closely related unless a third person is present.

According to Islamic understanding marriage is a private contract concluded between the bride (or her representative) and the groom (or his representative). This legal relationship can be terminated by either party, though usually the husband, through divorce (*talaq*) in court: "What God hates above all permitted things is deserting one's wife." However, a husband can always declare divorce unilaterally. The wife may also do so only if she has included the right in the marriage contract. A clause found in most marriage contracts pays only part of the dowry at the time of marriage; the greatest portion is paid out only in case of divorce. This is intended to protect the woman. The wife can also demand a divorce if the husband commits adultery or does not meet his marriage and support obligations. If there was nothing about divorce in the marriage contract, the woman can end her marriage—without any legal rights—only by leaving the house of her husband once and for all.

As a rule the marriage is performed by the imam, and now this often follows the civil ceremony in countries that require it. The newly married woman often has a difficult position in the traditional extended family. She is only recognized socially once she has become a mother, and particularly when she has sons. Later, when she becomes a grandmother, she gains the respect of her sons and all younger women in the family, especially the daughters-in-law. One could speak of a "mother-in-law order."

## MORE RECENT DEVELOPMENTS

Changes are coming to many Muslim societies, and with them there is tension between traditional and modern ways. This is the case with Turkey in particular. There, in rural areas, the sensitivity to honor and shame still plays a controlling role as a concern of the entire family, sometimes to the extent of a blood feud. This attitude is emphasized religiously: Honor and shame are seen respectively as earned worth or sin before God. The traditional religious law continues to exert a great deal of influence in such a traditional environment, yet Islamic law in Turkey was officially replaced by a secular civil law upon the separation of church and state (1926). In contemporary Turkish marriage law, polygamy is forbidden, monogamy and civil marriage are required by law, and divorce is possible for a woman.

The thought and behavior of people in Turkey are also undergoing profound change. The nuclear family is taking the place of the traditional extended family in rural areas as well as in the cities. It remains connected, however, in a web of blood ties. Care and responsibility for one another as well as mutual control are still effective. Changes in the position of women are coming about as increasing numbers of women hold jobs and earn their own money. But the conception is still widespread that women should work for pay only in emergency situations.

Such developments are taking place not only in Turkey, but in the entire Islamic world. In other Islamic countries, however, the prescriptions of Islamic law have much greater validity. Still, a clause can be inserted into a marriage contract giving the wife the power to get a divorce and to achieve a separation with compensation. Sometimes a contract can also stipulate that before the husband marries other wives, the first wife must agree.

Traditional attitudes and behaviors are questioned everywhere today. Many families experience difficult conflicts as a result. Islamic scholars have various reactions to these conflicts. Many advocate holding on to the traditional order because it is intended to be valid for all time. Others refer to the position of the woman in early Islam. Some Muslims promote complete equality for women in education and in societal positions.

## THE MINORITY SITUATION

When Muslim families live as a minority in a non-Islamic environment, the tensions are intensified between the traditional Islamic understanding of marriage and family and the attitudes and expectations of the new environment. These tensions are often expressed in severe conflicts between parents and the younger generation. In an unfamiliar environment, traditional values and close family relations are particularly important. At the same time, youth are pressured to conform to the culture around them and have a difficult time withdrawing from the attraction of the new ways of living.

Even among the secularized Turks, upon marriage the woman still joins the family of her husband. Thus religious law and common practice remain influential. This is also evident in religious mixed marriages when a Muslim man marries a non-Muslim woman. He is required to allow his wife to practice her religion. A Muslim woman, however, is forbidden to marry a non-Muslim who does not convert to Islam. Among other things, as a non-Muslim he is under no compulsion to allow her to practice her religion.

Girls are often expected to carry on the customs of their home country when living elsewhere, even if that means disadvantages for their education and career. For example, many parents forbid their daughters all contact with boys and participation in school activities that might conflict with traditional practices. Still, some traditional parents want their daughters to get good educations. The Qur'an and sunna call on all Muslims to seek knowledge everywhere and at all times.

A Muslim wife often experiences double isolation in a minority situation. In a non-Islamic country she can hardly find the security she had in the traditional society at home. If her husband works outside the home, she is cut off from outside contact. Other women, primarily if they are working, have emancipated themselves considerably.

Many Muslims have a hard time with such changes. The degree of difficulty depends on their response toward the new environment, whether it leads to disappointments and entrenchments, or to openness to new ways of living together.

# 7

# Death and Eternal Life,
# Dying and Burial

## CREATION AND RESURRECTION

The primary prayer of Islam (Sura 1) praises God as "Cherisher and Sustainer of the Worlds: Most Gracious, Most Merciful," and as "Master of the Day of Judgment." This reminds Muslims in every traditional prayer that all of life is directed toward the day of reward for good deeds and punishment for evil deeds. Accordingly, the list of six faith statements of Islam includes "I believe in God, his angels, his books, and his prophets" as well as "I believe in the last judgment and the predestination of good and evil from God." From the start the earliest summons of the Qur'an directed people to the inescapable judgment, "Verily, to thy Lord is the return (of all)" (Sura 96.8).

When God created humans, he equipped them with a sense of responsibility. They are to lead their lives in obedience to God's order, for they are intended to be God's representatives on earth, to whom the goods of the world are on loan from God for a time: "He who created Death and Life, that He may try which of you is

best in deed" (Sura 67.2). At the judgment God requires an ac-
counting from everyone.

According to the Qur'an, the creation of heaven and earth as
well as the change of day and night are indications that God is
leading the world order to the day of the resurrection of the dead,
and through the judgment to a new existence. For as God was and
is the creator of life, so he will also be on that day. "It is He who
begins (the process of) creation; then repeats it; and for Him it is
most easy" (Sura 30.27). The Qur'an speaks more than seventy
times of this approaching day.

Having heard about the judgment, people behave wisely
when they heed the warnings and instructions of God's prophets
in view of that great day. For everyone who is ungrateful for God's
blessings, lives selfishly, and follows only his or her own wishes,
the day of judgment will bring "Noise and Clamour" (Sura 101:1)
and "evil will be the morning" (Sura 37.177). But for those who
submit to God's will, he will lead them to the entrance of the "Home
of Peace" (Sura 10.25). To them it is said, "on the Day of Judgment
[you shall] be paid your full recompense" (Sura 3.185), "a goodly
(reward)—yea, more (than in measure)!" (Sura 10.26). For they
already thank God in this world, submit themselves to him in
prayer, and allow themselves to be directed by the Qur'an. Although Muslims are convinced that their way is the best, they
recognize that Jews and Christians, as those among the "people of
the book," can also count on God's mercy. For it is valid for all to
"strive together (as in a race) towards all that is good" (Sura 2.148)
in accordance with the directions (sharia) and ways God gave to
each of the three religions, until his decision at the last day
(Sura 5.48).


## DEATH AND JUDGMENT

"The Angel of Death, put in charge of you, will (duly) take your
souls" (Sura 32.11). Tradition further says that the two angels,
popularly named as Munkar and Nakir, will test the one who has
died with three questions at the grave, namely, "Who is your God?

Who is your prophet? What is your faith?" For those who give the right answers, some other angels will make the wait for the day of judgment easier. Those who give the wrong answers will begin to suffer punishment while awaiting the resurrection. Only those who die as martyrs in the faith or in "holy war" (*jihad*) go directly to paradise.

Similar to descriptions in the Bible, the Qur'an describes the day of judgment with cosmic catastrophes suddenly affecting the world. There is no escape from the judging God: Everyone will have to give account for what he or she has done or left undone. The Qur'an makes frequent use of images; for example, it says that human activities are penned down in books (Sura 84:6-8), and that good and evil deeds are weighed against each other on scales (23.102-103). God's judgment cannot be influenced; no intercessions are of any help before him. Many Muslims believe that not even the intercession of one of the prophets would help; on the other hand, the prophets—including Jesus—can serve as witnesses of complaint against their followers if they turn away from the path shown to them. But God has the freedom to forgive, for he is "the Forgiver" of faults, as Sura 40 says.

## PARADISE

Whoever passes God's judgment is counted among "the Companions of the Right Hand" (Sura 56.8) and may enter paradise. The Qur'an describes life in paradise in concrete terms: full of peace and security, without rancor and toil (Sura 15.45-48); for God's mercy determines everything. But the most precious gift in paradise is God's nearness. Hence in paradise there are faces that "beam (in brightness and beauty)—looking towards their Lord" (Sura 75:22-23), whose brilliance would be more than the human eye could bear. These statements are of great importance, especially for mystics.

Quite a few Muslims are convinced that hell will not be the end. They point to God's complete power and mercy (Sura 11.107-108). The Islamic tradition includes an old *hadith*, according to which

a day comes in hell when the gates swing in the wind as in an
abandoned house with no one left inside.


## DYING AND BURIAL

The Islamic understanding of death as a passage to judgment and
the beyond is reflected in the companionship afforded the dying
one and in the burial customs.

*On dying:* It is seen as a self-evident obligation and a good work
not to leave dying persons alone in the last hours. During this time,
friends and relatives remind them of all the good that God has
allowed them to experience. They should leave the world thankful.
Those present also ask God for forgiveness for all the errors in
which the dying person was entangled, confident that such a petition has great importance. Naturally they try to alleviate the suffering of the dying person, especially thirst.

If those present notice that the end is nearing, they try to turn
the dying person to face Mecca. Then they repeat the faith confession again and again, hoping that the dying person can whisper
or think along with them. The confession *Ash-hadu la ilaha illa Llah,*
"I confess that there is no God but Allah," ought to be the dying
person's last words.

*Bathing the dead:* According to Islamic understanding, bathing of
the dead should be done as soon as possible so that the deceased
person can rest. The rites of burial begin with bathing. Rules for
this are precisely laid out as a complete ritual bath. In the case of
a woman it is carried out by women, generally the next of kin, and
in the case of a man, by men, also relatives. At the beginning,
when it is announced that the bathing of the dead is taking place,
the *basmalah,* "in the name of God" is pronounced. Thus it is a
religious activity that can only be carried out by Muslims and may
not be neglected.

After bathing, the body is carefully wrapped in white linen
or cotton. This makes the dead person look like the pilgrims in the

holy district of Mecca. The white cloths symbolize complete dedication to God. Now the death prayer can begin, followed immediately by burial. A casket is not generally used in Islamic countries. If one is required, as it is in some Western countries, it should be as simple as possible.

*The death prayer:* For the death prayer, spoken in Arabic, the person leading the prayer steps behind the dead person, facing Mecca just like the dead person, who has been turned on his or her right side. The mourning community stands behind in rows of three. The death prayer itself is relatively short and is said while standing, without prostrating (*sajdah*). It is articulated through repeating the brief confession (called the *takbir*) four times, *Allahu akbar,* "God is greater than everything."

- After the first *takbir* the prayer of the Al-Fatiha (Sura 1) is spoken.
- The second *takbir* followed by a petition for the blessing of Abraham, also familiar from the daily traditional prayer: "O God, bless Mohammed and all who belong to him, as you blessed Abraham and his people. Bless them on all the earth. You are to be praised. You are the most high."
- After the third *takbir* comes a prayer or petition for the deceased. One may pray, "God forgive us, who live, and the one who died, forgive us young and old, men and women, present and absent. God, whoever among us you let live, let live as Muslims; and whoever you let die, let die in the faith." At this point prayers are said for the one who has died, "O God, forgive this dead person."
- After the fourth *takbir*, the opportunity is offered to say further free prayers in silence, similar to those after the third *takbir*.

The death prayer concludes like every traditional prayer, with the peace greeting, *As-salamu alaykum wa rahmatu-Llah* ("Peace be with you and God's mercy!"). Spoken by the imam, it is quietly repeated by all, turning first to the right and then to the left.

*The burial:* It is the duty of the men to bury the dead. Women take a peripheral role at most. The dead person is carried to the grave site by as many bearers as possible. People take turns in order to honor the dead and to give many the opportunity to do a good work. In the grave the dead person must lie on the right side with the face turned toward Mecca. On lowering the body these words are said: "In the name of God and according to the order of community of his followers." Once the body is positioned correctly, everyone helps to fill the grave with earth. While the first shovels of earth are falling, Sura 20.55 is quoted: "From the (earth) did We create you, and into it shall We return you, and from it shall We bring you out once again."

Tradition reports that Muhammad buried his daughter in this manner.

*The graves:* Muslim graves should be made simply, without stone framing or cover, and without flowers. A simple pillar can serve as grave decoration. Turning the graves toward Mecca is required. This makes it advisable to provide Muslims in other countries with their own burial sections in cemeteries. It would be helpful to arrange special rooms in funeral homes or elsewhere appropriate for bathing the dead.

Visits to the grave are intended as a reminder of one's own mortality and death rather than as an occasion to mourn and intercede for the dead. "For whoever thinks much at the grave will find a river of paradise. But whoever forgets will find the grave of hell," warns the respected theologian Al-Ghazzali.

## PART TWO

# Islam in North America
## by Paul Varo Martinson

# 8

# How Islam Came to North America

Islam is an increasing presence in North America, particularly in the United States. This growing community draws largely on two sources: African Americans who convert to Islam through the outreach of groups such as the former American Muslim Mission or through groups of uncertain Muslim character such as the "Black Muslims," or the Nation of Islam; and, secondly, immigrant peoples of nations with large Muslim populations in the Middle East, Asia, and Africa, and now also eastern Europe. In addition, small numbers of Anglos have converted to one form or another of Islam.[1]

The actual number of Muslims in the United States is still a disputed figure, with much depending on how one defines "Muslim." A recent, quite thorough study offers the figure of 4 million, with nearly one-third of these in the three states of California (more than 500,000), New York (400,000), and Illinois (170,000). It describes Islam as "the fastest growing religion in the United States today," soon to exceed the Jewish community of nearly 6 million, or 3 percent of the population.[2] In this case it seems to include in "Muslim" both estimated membership in African American Muslim

groups and all immigrants of Muslim origin whether or not they
are actively Muslim. Another recent study suggests a much more
modest figure of 1.4 million, or 0.05 percent of the U.S. population.
In this case the definition of "Muslim" seems to be those who
actively practice Islam.[3] In rough figures, about two-thirds of the
4 million are immigrant and one-third indigenous, with Anglo converts constituting only about 75,000 of this last group.[4] Immigration
continues apace at about 25,000 to 30,000 per year.[5] Of the immigrant population it is estimated that 80 to 90 percent of second-
and third-generation Muslims are unmosqued.[6]

Regardless of how one defines the term "Muslim" and the
figures one arrives at, it is a fact that Islam is a growing and living
presence within the United States, contributing a significant religious community to the increasingly pluralistic religious complex-
ion of the nation. Part 2 of this book will consider the history of
American Muslims, their self-understanding and place within
American society, and their relations with the Christian community.


## BEGINNINGS

The earliest presence of Muslims in the New World was apparently
that of "Moriscos"[7] who came with the Spanish ships, perhaps even
with Columbus himself.[8] Later, Muslims were among the invol-
untary immigrants, black slaves. One estimate, based on a detailed
analysis, is that as many as 30,000 African Muslims were brought
as slaves to the United States prior to the Civil War. There are
numerous evidences of Muslims among the slave population, including slaves who knew the entire Qur'an by heart.[9] Nevertheless,
as a result of the policy of dispersing slaves who came from a given
area or spoke a common language as a precaution against any kind
of revolt under religious or other auspices,[10] the Muslim faith was
not transmitted to future generations.

The first wave of voluntary Muslim immigrants (almost entirely from the Middle East and triggered by worsening economic
conditions partly stimulated by the altered economic configuration
after the opening of the Suez Canal in 1869) began around 1875

and continued through 1912. These immigrants were largely from the mountainous areas of Lebanon.[11] They had been preceded by Christian Arabs from Lebanon who had reportedly experienced financial success in the United States. Largely uneducated and unskilled, they settled mainly in or near industrial areas, becoming laborers, peddlers, factory workers, miners, and shopkeepers.[12] Many returned home, but those who remained in the United States found it difficult to integrate into American society and so formed close-knit communities. Subsequent to this, several other waves of Muslim immigration occurred. With the breakup of the Ottoman Empire after World War I and the imposition of French and English colonialism on the Middle East, a fresh wave came in 1918. By far the largest number were Lebanese Muslims who came between 1918 and 1922 to work in the Ford Rouge plant in Dearborn, Michigan. This surge was partly in anticipation of harsher immigration laws passed in 1921 and particularly in 1924,[13] which applied highly restrictive quotas to non-northern European peoples. The 1930s saw a third wave. During these several waves the growth was largely by chain immigration, the coming of relatives of earlier immigrants as allowed by U.S. immigration laws.

The circle widened considerably after World War II with the fourth wave beginning in 1947 and running through the 1950s. Three great movements of people to the United States in the postwar period—the flocking of students to American universities, the "brain drain" of professionals from lesser-developed countries, and the flight of refugees from political and religious oppression—contributed to an exponential growth of Islam in the United States. Moreover, immigration laws had been liberalized. Now Muslims also came from Asia, especially India and Pakistan, from eastern Europe and the Soviet Union, as well as from Africa and elsewhere. The political uncertainties and unavoidable dislocations spawned by independence in the postcolonial period accounted for the coming of many from former European colonies. A large percentage of these refugees came from educated and professional classes; they also tended to emphasize the rational aspect of Islam as a religion of ethical responsibility rather than a religion that stressed law and ritual. A similar kind of elite together with some semiskilled workers came with the fifth wave from 1967 on. Many now came from Iran, especially after the revolution there in 1979.[14] There was also an influx of Muslims who received financial support from Saudi Arabia, and who generally represent the more conservative law- and ritual-oriented "official" Islam.[15] Some sixty nations are represented today in the Muslim immigrant communities of North America.[16] They constitute per capita the most highly educated Muslim population in the world.[17]

## ISLAM AMONG AFRICAN AMERICANS

About the time of the first wave of Muslim immigration, Islamic ideas began to have a fitful start within the African American community, giving rise to a number of proto-Muslim[18] groups. In an 1888 book, Edward Wilmot Blyden unfavorably contrasted the racial impact of Christianity on Africans with what he considered a more racially harmonious Islam.[19] This attitude, among other things, contributed to a predisposition for African Americans to turn to Islam rather than Christianity in the search for greater freedom and dignity.

In the early part of this century (1913) Noble Drew Ali began his Moorish Science movement and established a temple in Newark, New Jersey. An African American hailing from North Carolina, he sensed the power of symbolism and concluded that the black man's humiliation was all in the names given to them by others. Apparently without formal education, he nevertheless had some acquaintance with oriental thought and knew that Islam had been the religion of North Africans, or the Moors. He was also acquainted with revivalist Christianity. Noble Drew Ali spun a web of mythology that made the African American of one stock with the Asiatics. In this redefinition, he taught, they had recovered their lost identity, which somehow was equivalent to being Moorish American. Identity cards were issued to each follower and some externals of Islam appropriated: display of the Qur'an, wearing of fezzes, Muslim names, repudiation of Christian beliefs. Included in the beliefs was expectation of the imminent destruction of the white race. As time went on a power struggle ensued, resulting in his death in 1929. The movement fractured into numerous sub-groups and lost influence within the African American community. The small group that continues to follow his teachings believes him to be reincarnate in their present leaders.[20]

The African American community was a highly alienated segment of the U.S. population. For instance, even though they had fought for democracy in World War I, African American soldiers returned home to experience bigotry once more. Within a year of the end of the war, seventy blacks were lynched, many of them still in uniform. Fourteen others were burned publicly, eleven of these burned alive. In 1919 race riots erupted across the country. Out of this maelstrom of oppression and resentment, the extreme black nationalist Garveyite movement exploded on the scene, up to the time "the largest mass movement in the history of the American Negro."[21] The Garveyite movement itself included the trappings of Christianity in its ideology. Nevertheless, it was this quest for a black national identity in the face of oppression, combined with the prestige of Islam as an alternative to Christian domination, that led to the subsequent Black Muslim movement.[22]

## THE NATION OF ISLAM

Elijah Poole was born in Sandersville, Georgia, in 1897, son of an itinerant Baptist preacher. What he learned of Islam was gleaned from a mysterious Wallace D. Fard who appeared amid the African American community of Detroit in the summer of 1930. A peddler of uncertain origin, but thought by some to be an Arab, Fard sold his wares and gradually his ideas, holding meetings in homes. He began with the Bible as a textbook but gradually weaned his followers from it to his own ideas. He spoke of dietary laws, denounced the white race, spelled out the glories of Black Afro-Asia, and eventually attacked the Bible itself. The movement grew and a hall was hired and called the Temple of Islam. An early convert quotes Fard as saying: "My name is W. D. Fard, and I come from the Holy City of Mecca. More about myself I will not tell you yet, for the time has not yet come. I am your brother. You have not yet seen me in my royal robes."[23] He announced himself to the Detroit police as "the supreme Ruler of the Universe." With the securing of the temple, a tightly knit organization began to develop, strict rules of acceptance into the movement were devised, and a hierarchy formed. Fard also attracted followers of Noble Drew Ali. C. Eric Lincoln sums up the subsequent development:

> Within three years, Fard had developed an organization so effective that he was able to withdraw almost entirely from active leadership. He had not only set up the temple and established its ritual and worship but also founded a University of Islam (actually, a combined elementary and secondary school), dedicated to "higher mathematics," astronomy and the "ending of the spook civilization." He had created the Muslim Girls Training Class, which taught young Muslim women the principles of home economics and how to be a proper wife and mother. Finally, "fear of trouble with unbelievers, especially with the police, led to the founding of the Fruit of Islam—a military organization for the men who were drilled by captains and taught tactics and the use of firearms." A Minister of Islam was now appointed to run the entire organization, aided by a staff of assistant ministers. Each of these men was selected and trained personally by Fard, who gradually stopped his public appearances and eventually disappeared from view.[24]

Fard had selected Elijah Poole, whom he renamed Elijah Muhammad, to preside over the movement of about eight thousand followers. And, "the choice proved a wise one. Elijah Muhammad was almost single-handedly responsible for the deification of Fard and for the perpetuation of his teachings in the early years after Fard disappeared"[25] in the summer of 1934. Forced by factionalism to leave Detroit, Elijah Muhammad set up his headquarters at Temple No. 2 in Chicago, where he became the "Prophet" of Allah, the latter now identified with Fard. He built up a cohesive, aggressive movement that gave his followers a newfound sense of dignity, built up their economy, and gave them hope not only as equal with but superior to the white race and destined to rule the earth. Within two or three decades the movement grew to include 100,000 or more.

We have spoken of the movement as proto-Muslim. While it shares some ideas with Islam generally—acceptance of the Qur'an, belief in one God (Allah)—it includes many others that are distinctly non-Islamic. The non-Islamic ideas include Fard as a manifestation of Allah; Elijah Muhammad as Allah's last messenger; God as not spirit but human and black; heaven and hell on earth at this time with no life after death; seven daily prayers; and fasting during the month of December.[26] Its explicitly racist doctrine—the origins of humanity as Black Man; the demonization of the white race that was created by an evil black scientist, Yakub, who removed their humanity; and the subsequent six-thousand-year rule of the world by the white race and its now impending doom to be replaced by legitimate black rule—constitutes "the central myth" of the Nation of Islam.[27] As preparatory steps in bringing about the future of black rule, a rigorous moral code and orderly way of life exemplified in the paramilitary Fruit of Islam were implemented, a call was issued for a separate black nation within the United States, and an aggressive program to develop an independent African American economy (from farming to retail business) was put into place. Among other things, these measures promoted a sense of cohesion, dignity, and purpose among the followers as well as contributed to dramatic changes in the socioeconomic conditions of the members of the Nation.[28]

Nevertheless, the Nation of Islam was an unstable mixture of myth and reality. One of its most notable leaders, Malcolm X, was disillusioned by the disclosure of moral misconduct by Elijah Muhammad and left the movement to found his own Muslim Mosque, Inc. in 1964. Shortly thereafter, upon pilgrimage to Mecca, Malcolm X became disabused of the racist doctrines of the movement, finding Islam to be a religion of racial harmony. As he put it, while on pilgrimage, "I lay awake amid sleeping Muslim brothers and I learned that pilgrims from every land—every color, and class, and rank; high officials and beggars alike—all snored in the same language."[29] He thus withdrew from the movement and moved closer to orthodox Islam, taking the name of El-Hajj Malik El-Shabazz, only to be assassinated shortly thereafter, February 21, 1965.[30] Meanwhile Elijah Muhammad's son, Wallace Deen, traveled to the

Middle East and studied at Al-Azhar Mosque in Cairo. There he learned the true teachings of Islam and embraced them. Upon the death of Elijah Muhammad on February 25, 1975, Deen was confirmed by a gathering of 20,000 members the next day as the Chief Minister of the Nation of Islam,[31] becoming the effective leader of a religious empire worth some sixty to eighty million dollars.[32] He immediately commenced a series of major reforms in the movement, well summarized by Lincoln:

> The catalogue of changes Wallace has accomplished in only five years of leadership tenure is already long and detailed. There have been changes of doctrine, changes of structure and administration, changes of name, style, role, and office. There were changes of official attitude about race, political involvement, and military service. High-ranking members of the ruling hierarchy were demoted or reassigned; financing of the movement's super-structure was redesigned and a strict accounting system introduced. The Fruit of Islam was disbanded. Key elements underpinning Elijah Muhammad's mythological doctrines were either allegorized, reinterpreted, or quietly abandoned altogether, and the "blue-eyed arch-enemy," that is, the "white devils," were rehabilitated and welcomed into the movement as brothers.[33]

In one fell swoop, the movement was brought into the mainstream of Islam. Its principal organ was changed from *Muhammad Speaks* to *The Bilalian News* and later again to *The Muslim Journal*, while the name of the movement itself underwent changes. First it became The World Community of al-Islam in the West (WCI) and the believers designated Bilalians (after the name of the former Ethiopian slave who became the first muezzin, caller to prayer, in Muhammad's Medinan community) in 1976. It was changed again in 1980 to The American Muslim Mission; both organization and name were abandoned by 1985. It was time for the African American Muslim to integrate into Islam generally, though Wallace Deen still heads a movement and publishes *The Muslim Journal*. Wallace himself changed his name to Warith to distance himself from his namesake Wallace Fard. As evidence of his acceptance into the worldwide Muslim community, he was the only American invited to observe the Tenth Annual Islamic Conference of Ministers of Foreign Affairs in Fez, Morocco, and in 1978 was designated by Saudi Arabia, Abu Dhabi, and Qatar as the "sole consultant and trustee" for the recommendation and distribution of funds to Muslim organizations dedicated to the propagation of Islam in the United States. These dramatic changes have been accompanied by considerable strain. Louis Farrakhan led the major schismatic movement of about a thousand that returned to the original teachings and practices of Elijah Muhammad. In 1993 Farrakhan's followers numbered perhaps twenty thousand.[34]

While the Nation of Islam and its successor groups (including the Hanafi movement headed by Hamaas Abdul Khaalis, who seceded from the Nation of Islam in the early 1960s) have had by far the greatest impact on the African American population, there have been other Muslim influences as well. One of these is the unorthodox Muslim movement of the Ahmadiyya (see page 135).

## NOTES

1. Most Anglo converts are either women who have married Muslim men and have converted, or students, who tend to be attracted to various Sufi groups. See Yvonne Haddad, "Muslims in the United States," in *Islam: The Religious and Political Life of a World Community*, ed. Marjorie Kelly (New York: Praeger, 1984), 258–74; and Earle Waugh, "Muslim Leadership and the Shaping of the Umma: Classical Tradition and Religious Tension in the North American Setting," in *The Muslim Community in North America*, ed. Earle H. Waugh et al. (Edmonton: University of Alberta Press, 1983), 26, 32 n. 39. According to Nadim Makdisi, the first known American to convert to Islam was Mohammed Alexander Russel Webb, a journalist who entered diplomatic service in 1887 as the American consul in Manila. He was converted by Indian Muslims there. On his return to the United States, he founded the Oriental Publishing Company in New York City and published the first issue of *Moslem World* in 1893. See Emily Kalled Lovell, "Islam in the United States: Past and Present," in *The Muslim Community*, 99; and Nadim Makdisi, "The Moslems in America," *The Christian Century* 76:34 (26 Aug. 1959): 969.

2. Carol L. Stone, "Estimate of Muslims Living in America," in *The Muslims of America*, ed. Yvonne Y. Haddad (New York: Oxford University Press, 1991), 25–36. It should be noted that no official government statistics on Muslims exist, inasmuch as the last religious census was in 1936, and

even in that census Muslims were not counted. See Lovell, "Islam in the United States," 94. In fact, estimates range from the exaggerated figure of 9 million (the 1993 *World Almanac* gives 8 million) to the parsimonious 600,695. See Yvonne Y. Haddad and Adair T. Lummis, *Islamic Values in the United States* (New York: Oxford University Press, 1987), 173. On Jewish population see *Statistical Abstract of the United States* (Washington, D.C.: Bureau of Census, Department of Commerce, 1987), 52.

3. *New York Times*, 10 April 1991, A-11. This reports a survey commissioned by the Graduate School of the City University of New York. It extrapolated from a survey of 113,000 people around the nation. Another contemporaneous study, B. Kosmin and J. Scheckner, *Estimating the Muslim Population in the United States in 1990* (New York: CUNY Graduate Center, 17 Jan. 1991), comes up with a similar figure of 1.5 million, even though using a different method. According to this study, 800,000 Muslims are of the immigrant population, 300,000 African American, 100,000 Anglo converts, and 80,000 students. See Aryeh Meir and Reuven Firestone, *Islam in America* (New York: American Jewish Committee, Institute of Human Relations, 1992), 19, 28 n. 5.

4. Most of these are white female spouses of Muslim men and a few whites who convert to one or another neo-Sufi group. Haddad, "Muslims in the United States," 258.

5. Haddad and Lummis, *Islamic Values*, 3, 173.

6. Ibid., 8. According to another reckoning, only between 1 and 5 percent of immigrant Muslims attend the mosque. See Yvonne Y. Haddad, "The Muslim Experience in the United States," *The Link* 2:4 (Sept.–Oct. 1979): 10.

7. These were Muslims in Spain forcibly converted to Christianity, many of them superficially. See also Betty Patchin Green, "The Alcaldes of California," in *Aramco World Magazine* (Nov.–Dec. 1976): 26–29, on a quasi-Islamic legal institution, the *alcaldes*, brought into the earliest settlements in California.

8. Beverlee Turner Mehdi notes a report that Columbus took a Louis de Torre to act as Arabic interpreter when he reached Muslim India. De Torre was a Moor who had recently converted to Christianity and taken a Christian name. Moorish rule in Granada, the last stronghold of Islam in western Europe, was brought to an end in 1492. See Beverlee Turner Mehdi, ed., *The Arabs in America 1492–1977: A Chronology and Fact Book* (Dobbs Ferry, N.Y.: Oceana Publications, 1978), 1.

9. The most celebrated case in this last regard was that of Job ben Solomon from Gambia, sold in Annapolis in 1731. See the fascinating account and detailed documentation of a number of such Muslim slaves in Allan D. Austin, *African Muslims in Antebellum America: A Sourcebook* (New York: Garland Publishing, 1984). For Job's story see p. 73. James A.

Michener comments thus on Alex Haley's novel, *Roots:* "To have Kunta Kinte, or one of his fellows, praying to Allah while chained in the bottom of a Christian ship is an unjustified sop to contemporary developments rather than true reflection of the past" ("*Roots,* Unique in its Time," *New York Times Book Review* 26 [Feb. 1977]: 41). In his reference to contemporary developments, Michener has in mind Haley's composition of Malcolm X's autobiography (see n. 29 below). Austin's book is a detailed demonstration of the realism of Haley's fictional hero. Austin comments: "The absence of any criticism of Michener's comment may indicate how ignorant of Africa, and Islam, the people of the United States still are" (p. 4). This does not mean that *Roots* is not without its failure in historical realism. See, for instance, p. 117, n. 65 in Austin's book. See also Clyde-Ahmad Winters, "Afro-American Muslims from Slavery to Freedom," *Islamic Studies* 17:4 (1978): 190–205, also 187–90. For other accounts of early nonslave Muslims, see Makdisi, "The Moslems in America," 969–71.

10. C. Eric Lincoln, "The American Muslim Mission in the Context of American Social History," in *The Muslim Community,* 215–33. Such a revolt had taken place among black slaves in Brazil.

11. See, for instance, Yvonne Haddad, "Arab Muslims and Islamic Institutions in America: Adaptation and Reform," in *Arabs in the New World: Studies on Arab-American Communities,* ed. Sameer Y. Abraham and Nabeel Abraham (Detroit: Wayne State University, Center for Urban Studies, 1983), 65–66.

12. Successful though they may have been, it is estimated that by 1914, fully 90 percent of Syrian immigrants, as they were called, were peddlers. See Deborah L. Miller, "Middle Easterners: Syrians, Lebanese, Armenians, Egyptians, Iranians, Palestinians, Turks, Afghans," in (*They Chose Minnesota: A Survey of the State's Ethnic Groups,* ed. June Drenning Holmquist (St. Paul: Minnesota Historical Society Press, 1981), 514f.

13. The period 1917 to 1964 can be designated "The Era of Restriction" in U.S. immigration policy. The Immigration Act of 1917 required a literacy test before immigrants could enter. Those who failed were returned. The 1921 Quota Act limited the annual number of entrants from admittable nationalities to 3 percent of the foreign-born total of that nationality based on the 1910 census. Restrictionists pushed for the even more restrictive 1924 Immigration Act, which reduced the admissible yearly total to 165,000 and national quotas to 2 percent based on the 1890 census. It also provided for a "national origins" system that favored northern and western Europe. This favoritism replaced the quota system in 1927. These and similar restrictive policies prevailed until 1965, when the Hart-Celler Act began a process of liberalization. See Stephan Thernsten, ed., *Harvard Encyclopedia of American Ethnic Groups* (Cambridge, Mass.: Harvard University Press, 1980), 492–95.

14. As many as 250,000 Iranians opposed to the Khomeini regime came at this time, many of whom were students. Haddad, "Muslims in the United States," 271. In 1979 it was estimated that there were 750,000 Muslim foreign students in the U.S. from all countries. See Haddad, "The Muslim Experience in the United States," 1–12.

15. Haddad and Lummis, *Islamic Values*, 13–14, 157.

16. Ibid., 3. The non-Arabs are largely from Pakistan, Iran, Afghanistan, Turkey, and eastern Europe.

17. Ibid., 5.

18. I borrow this term from Lincoln, "The American Muslim Mission," 224.

19. Edward Wilmot Blyden (1832–1912), *Christianity, Islam, and the Negro Race*, 2d ed. (London: W. B. Whittingham & Co., 1988.) He cites approvingly, for instance, these words of Bosworth Smith: "Christian travellers, with every wish to think otherwise, have remarked that the Negro who accepts Mohammedanism acquires at once a sense of the dignity of human nature not commonly found even among those who have been brought to accept Christianity." Blyden himself comments (pp. 11–12) on the "servility" of the Christian Negro in contrast to the "self-reliant, productive, independent, and dominant" spirit of Muslim Negroes.

20. His dates are 1886–1929. See, for instance, C. Eric Lincoln, *The Black Muslims in America* (Boston: Beacon Press, 1961), 50–55.

21. At about the same time, Marcus Garvey came on the scene. From Jamaica, he had developed the idea of creating a Universal Negro Improvement Association (UNIA) in 1914. In 1916 he began preaching in New York. He traveled through thirty-eight states to study the plight of the American Negro. His vision enlarged as he began to contemplate the uniting of the world's 400 million Negroes that would give them a common political identity. His newspaper, *The Negro World*, was printed in several languages and was said to have a circulation of 200,000 or more. The First International Convention of UNIA was held in 1920. The trappings of government were developed: a "Declaration of the Rights of the Negro Peoples of the World," a flag, an order of nobility with honorary orders, salaries for leadership, election of Garvey as Provisional President of the African Republic, and so on. This militant black nationalist movement also took on the trappings of religion, worshiping a black God, drawing on the leadership of a renegade Episcopalian. The movement soon ran into all sorts of difficulties, including the energetic rejection of Garveyism by black intellectuals. Criminal charges involving misuse of funds and murder were eventually brought against Garvey and his followers. The U.S. government won a conviction and deported Garvey in 1927 since he was not a U.S. citizen. With that his movement faded. He died in 1940. See Lincoln, *The Black Muslims in America*, 56–66.

22. Apparently C. Eric Lincoln coined the term "Black Muslim" in describing the history of the Nation of Islam. The modifier "black" is used because the "Moors" among the Spanish conquistadores were the first to introduce Islam to this continent, the only Muslims in the New World were imported black slaves, and the more recently arrived immigrant Muslims grouped among themselves and did not reach out to Muslims of other ethnic groups. Lincoln, "The American Muslim Mission," 219.

23. Lincoln, *The Black Muslims in America*, 11. Fard drew ideas from several places, including the writings of Joseph F. "Judge" Rutherford (leader of the Jehovah's Witnesses), Hendrik Willem Van Loon's *Story of Mankind*, James Henry Breasted's *The Conquest of Civilization*, the Qur'an, the Bible, some literature of Freemasonry, and the addresses of Frank Norris (a Baptist fundamentalist preacher). Our account draws upon Lincoln.

24. Lincoln, *The Black Muslims in America*, 14.

25. Ibid., 15. Note also the strange uncertainties of Fard's disappearance.

26. See, for instance, Lovell, "Islam in the United States," 103. The basic creed or *shahada*, for instance, of the Nation of Islam is clearly heretical as far as Islam is concerned: "In the name of Allah who came in the person of Master Farad Muhammad, the Beneficient, the Merciful, the One God to whom all things are due, the Lord of the World and his Apostle, the Honourable Elijah Muhammad, the last of the Messengers of Allah." See Lawrence H. Mamiya, "Minister Louis Farrakhan and the Final Call: Schism in the Muslim Movement," in *The Muslim Community*, 240. On the mixed mind of immigrant Sunni or orthodox Muslims in relating to the Black Muslims, see *The Muslim Community*, p. 21f.

27. Lincoln, *The Black Muslims in America*, 76ff. On the subject of race in Islam proper, see Mamiya, "Minister Louis Farrakhan and Final Call," 253 n. 7.

28. Mamiya, "Minister Louis Farrakhan and the Final Call," 245ff.

29. Alex Haley and Malcolm X, *The Autobiography of Malcolm X* (New York: Grove Press, 1966), 344.

30. Even after his death, Malcolm X continues to wield a significant influence within the African American community, as witnessed in the dramatic response to Spike Lee's movie *Malcolm X*. See, for instance, the special report "Malcolm X: Finding the Man inside the Myth," *Newsweek* (16 Nov. 1992), 66–74.

31. Lincoln, "The American Muslim Mission," 228.

32. Mamiya, "Minister Louis Farrakhan and the Final Call," 245.

33. Lincoln, "The American Muslim Mission," 227.

34. See Mamiya, "Minister Louis Farrakhan and the Final Call," 234–55. Born in the Bronx, raised in Boston, Farrakhan had been influenced by Malcolm X to leave his profession as a violinist cum calypso singer. He

took over the mosque that Malcolm founded in Boston; after it split from the movement, he took over Malcolm's Temple No. 7 in Harlem, the most prestigious after the headquarters in Chicago. After Malcolm's death he assumed aspects of Malcolm's former role. On the size of Farrakhan's movement, see Don Terry, "Black Muslims Enter Islamic Mainstream," part 2 of "Muslims in America," *New York Times* (3 May 1993), A-9.

# 9

# Self-Understanding and Place in Society

A primary feature of the Islamic experience in North America is the fact that Muslims of whatever kind live in an essentially non-Muslim environment. That is to say, they do not live in the region of *dar al-Islam*, regions that are Muslim religiously, culturally, and politically, but in that of the *dar al-harb*—regions that, in the medieval schema, were un-Islamic and, whether because of persecuting Muslims or denying access to information about Islam, were subject to warfare. However it is understood, they live in an environment that in many ways seems hostile to living the Muslim life.

This particular sense of alienation from the wider environment is different for immigrant Muslims than it is for indigenous Muslims. For the latter, their Muslim faith has enabled them to overcome a sense of impotence and little worth even while continuing to protest the history of racial abuse and society's contemporary oppressions. In contrast, immigrant Muslims voluntarily came to these shores and often chose to leave a Muslim environment and dwell in a non-Muslim one. This was so because there seemed to be certain advantages to living in the context of a secular, democratic state. Nonetheless, for the conscientious immigrant Muslim a sense of estrangement from the environment persists.

In order to better understand the contemporary Muslim ethos in the United States, we shall examine the Muslim experience in terms of three classic concepts: *hijrah* (emigration), *jihad* (effort), and *dawah* (mission or calling).[1]

Emigration or *hijrah* is at the heart of the earliest Muslim experience. Because Muhammad was not accepted by his own people in Mecca as God's prophet, he and his followers emigrated to Medina in 622, the year from which Islamic calendars begin. There they were welcomed, and Islam as a coherent and organized religious-political community commenced.

Both the African American and immigrant Muslim communities have experienced a *hijrah* of sorts, though different from that of Muhammad. Perhaps that of the African American Muslims is more akin to that of Muhammad in that they have "exited," so to speak, from a dominant culture hostile to Islam by virtue of both its secularity and its pervasive Christian identity. In addition, it was the deeper hostility of racial and social oppression that most of all stimulated this exile. Elijah Muhammad sought before, as does Louis Farrakhan now, a literal exile by laying claim to a nation within a nation, a segregated realm. With Warith Deen, the goal became rather the forging of a Muslim identity in conformity with Islam around the world and in a way consistent with and strongly affirming of the secular political environment of the United States. In this regard, then, an African American may go through an emigration experience not entirely different from that of the actual modern immigrant.

As for the immigrant Muslim community, it is a fact that many of them left a Muslim environment that, for one reason or another, they found to be less hospitable for economic or professional advancement than the secular, democratic, Christian environment of the United States. This voluntary exile creates its own set of problems, including that of Muslim identity. At the same time, this kind of emigration is in many ways consistent with the pattern of the spread of Islam throughout history, where it has often been the

Muslim trader or merchant who has taken up domicile in an essentially non-Muslim environment and has thereby become over time the nucleus for a new Muslim community. In any case, indigenous and immigrant Muslims both experience to one degree or another existence within an often suspicious if not hostile environment.

For those committed to their faith, this situation can only mean exertion or effort, *jihad*. One of the basic commands of Allah in the Qur'an is to strive in the way of God. This struggle takes place at several levels: individual and personal, familial and social, institutional and national.

At the individual and personal level, the familiar difficulties are quickly evident. One can easily enough be a confessor of faith in the one God, but Islam is more than a confession, it is a way of life. It involves, for instance, prayer at the specified hours, and especially at Friday noon; it involves eating habits that include abstinence from alcoholic beverages and pork; it involves dress codes, especially on the part of females, as well as properly construed male-female relations in general. Workplace and professional obligations do not take into consideration the rigors the Muslim assumes during the month of fasting. In all of these areas, one's integrity as a Muslim is at stake. How can one be a true confessor of faith in the one God and yet be lax in these matters of obligatory individual behavior?

The difficulties become even more severe at the familial level. What about children in public schools, where boy-girl relations do not conform with Muslim standards, and where the values taught are often in direct conflict with Muslim values? What about the holidays, such as Easter and Christmas, which Muslims do not accept as their own and yet which attract their children and render traditional Islamic days of celebration less attractive? What about the relations of Muslim children with neighborhood children? How should Muslims deal with invitations into non-Islamic homes, with their non-Islamic eating and other habits? What about rules relating to marriage and divorce, inheritance, and the like? How is one to buy a house for one's family without engaging in the non-Muslim practice of borrowing and lending at interest? The tension between *hijrah* (the fact that they emigrated to a non-Muslim environment) and *jihad* (the committal to or effort of being Islamic) for the immigrant Muslim can be strongly felt, focused on the younger generation. As one Muslim put it: "The most important problem is with our young people. They are constantly confronted with western customs which are forbidden by the Qur'an—such as boys and girls playing sports together—yet these customs are very attractive to them. . . . Yet we have chosen this country, and we must learn to love it and participate fully in it."[2]


## MOSQUE COMMUNITIES

Ultimately these matters cannot be resolved simply at the individual or family level; they require effort at the institutional level. Initially the immigrant Muslim population was fragmented both because of scattered locations and because of diverse national provenance. The trend of many was toward assimilation.[3] Nevertheless, as the kinds of pressure identified above built up, together with the natural desire to associate with one's own kind, various Islamic institutions were established.

The single most important institutional development is the Islamic center or mosque community; that is, the cohesion of Muslims within a delimited geographical area about an Islamic center or mosque.[4] This development began in a small way in earlier years, but has burgeoned in the last decade or so. An early example was the Islamic Center that was incorporated in Michigan City, Indiana, by members of that area's largely Syrian and Lebanese Muslim population. In 1920 the Muslims of Cedar Rapids, Iowa, established the oldest existing mosque in the United States by converting a rented hall.[5] Plans were also laid to build a formal mosque, which was completed in 1933, and an imam from Saudi Arabia was hired to help in this development.[6] In 1945 ambitious plans were made for the formation of an Islamic Center in Washington, D.C., resulting in the Washington Mosque Foundation. Over time fourteen Muslim governments cooperated; the director's salary was paid on an ongoing basis by Egypt and the imams were supplied by Al-Azhar University in Cairo. The cornerstone for the mosque was laid in 1949; it was completed in 1957.[7] Also worthy of mention are the New York Mosque at Third Avenue and Ninety-sixth Street in Manhattan, which opened in April 1991; the new mosque being built in south-central Los Angeles for $8.5 million, mostly from Saudi funding;[8] and the gleaming mosque outside Toledo, Ohio. But whether large or small, as of 1987 the U.S. Muslim community, including both immigrant and indigenous, was served by 598 mosques and Islamic centers. At that time only the states of Alaska, Montana, South Dakota, and Wyoming were without one. At the time of writing (1993), the figure is given as 1,100 mosques, 80 percent of them established within the last twelve years.[9]

A mosque community typically comes into being through several stages. A group of families may come together for worship, moving from house to house. As the group enlarges, they may form a legal association and then rent a site that will more adequately serve their worship needs. Finally a building may be constructed dedicated to this purpose.[10] The formation of such a community can, however, be a complex matter. The immigrant communities may experience interethnic, international, and intergenerational tensions, as well as tensions between the more conservative and liberal perspectives. As one immigrant put it, after prayers "the Pakistanis return to their curries and the Arabs to their kebabs."[11] These tensions can be accentuated if the mosque community secures the services of an imam or prayer leader who may have definite ideas, perhaps of an extremely conservative cast. But in many if not most cases, the establishment of the mosque community is carried out by lay leaders of the community, not by professional religious leaders, who are in many cases not available.

The mosque traditionally performs many functions: the center of Islamic learning, locus of political activity, a place of rest from the stress of daily life, a place for experiencing community, and the like. Because of the isolation of the Muslim community within the American context, these functions can only expand, serving the community for everything from worship to recreation. Where an imam is present, his role likewise expands. Traditionally he is the person in the community thought to be best qualified through his knowledge of the Qur'an to be the Friday prayer service leader. He is not the equivalent of a pastor. In the United States, however, his role does take on pastoral-like responsibilities: visiting the sick and bereaved, counseling families, educating children, participating in ecumenical organizations, representing the community, conducting funerals and performing marriages, interpreting American society to the community, providing administrative expertise, and on and on. Thus the imam tends to take on the role of professional clergy.[12] The mosque or center may establish a Sunday school or, even more ambitiously, an Islamic school as an alternative to public school. In fact, it appears that the Muslim community, much like the Roman Catholic church earlier, is establishing a network of parochial schools. Currently there are some 165 full-time Muslim schools in the United States, even though 90 percent of Muslim children in the U.S. still go to public schools.[13]

## POLITICAL INVOLVEMENT

The sphere of political involvement encompasses local and national levels. Apart from the militancy of "black Muslims" in the past, Muslims, particularly immigrant Muslims, have been hesitant to enter into the political arena. For one thing, because of the high profile accorded to "Islamic fundamentalism" in the press and on television, overt public activity, particularly in the direction of Muslim causes, draws unwelcome attention. During the Persian Gulf War in 1991, for instance, one Muslim was refused passage on a Pan American flight because he held an Iraqi passport. In a subsequent interview by the local newspaper he "asked that his last name not be used because of threats . . . made against other Iraqis whose names have been published."[14]

To be sure, the Muslim community often responds with considerable ambiguity to international events involving Muslim states. There is nearly universal support for the Palestinian cause. So too has there been universal dismay at the inaction of Western nations in the face of atrocities against Bosnian Muslims. But other matters become more complex. During the Iranian hostage crisis of 1979–80, for instance, Muslims of Iranian extraction found "a new sense of unity, of pride, of identity." This was the case particularly for Iranian students, who felt a certain vindication in seeing Iran stand up to a superpower. With this sense of identity was mixed a sense of fear, so that they "considered it expedient during this time to present a low profile, to remain as anonymous as was possible."[15] This ambiguity is richly displayed by Mr. Alawan, a Shi'ite and a leader of the Muslim community in Dearborn, Michigan. Describing himself as a Goldwater Republican and "constitutional conservative," he at the same time spoke of Ayatollah Khomeini as a "pragmatist" while he sat under his picture, and spoke of Iran as the only genuine Muslim government around.[16] No doubt most Muslims would not agree.

Gradually Muslims are becoming increasingly active in both local and national politics. What will it mean should the Muslim community, soon to outgrow the Jewish community in size, become as active as the Jewish politically? Muslims fall on both sides of the political spectrum, some inclining toward Democratic and others toward Republican politics.[17] There is, however, a broader consensus that family issues are uppermost—issues involving abortion, homosexuality, sexual promiscuity, prayer in schools, drugs—and here the cast is clearly in the conservative direction. The American Muslim Council in Washington was founded in 1990 to encourage Muslims to become involved in local politics and to lobby for Muslim concerns.[18] Perhaps the first step leading to political involvement is advocacy for the Muslim community at the local level in the face of hostility or misunderstanding. Through talks at local churches and other organizations and through "letters to the editor," an effort to convey a truer picture of Islam is made, and a clear distinction drawn between genuine Islam and terrorist aberrations.

## OUTREACH TO OTHERS

Not only is the Muslim community concerned to gain an accepted and secure place within its new environment. For those who are most deeply committed to Islam, the Muslim obligation is far greater than that. Mission or calling, *dawah*, conveys something of this greater obligation to reach out to others. The call to prayer that Muslims traditionally hear five times a day is not simply a call to Muslims, but is implicitly a call to all peoples to come to the good, to come to faith in and obedience to Allah.[19]

This aspect of the Muslim commitment finds a number of expressions. Historically, the Muslim conquests of the seventh and eighth centuries created a setting that fostered the growth of Islam, but this political approach is hardly viable in North America. Historically, intermarriage has also been a powerful element in Muslim growth. Traditionally Muslim men can marry non-Muslim women, while the reverse is not acceptable. Nearly every Muslim community in North America has families in which the wife was originally Christian and who may or may not have converted to Islam, but whose children are given a Muslim upbringing. There is also an active effort to Islamize society, beginning with individual commitment. Here the hope is not only that each Muslim will become genuinely Muslim in his or her life and that Muslim families will become models for others to see what it is to be Muslim, but that a larger and growing Muslim community will be established that will eventually shape the entire sociopolitical environment.[20] In this sense each local mosque and Islamic center becomes a locus of mission. The late scholar Ism'ail R. Al-Faruqi was a vigorous exponent of this last approach. He writes:

> In North America, and the West generally, there is so much atheism, so much abnegation of religious truth, so much rejection of the most fundamental tenets of Judaism and Christianity, so much skepticism, as to arouse and shake the least sensitive religious conscience. The person endowed with the vision of Islam cannot witness the scene with indifference. Sooner or later, he must come to the realization that his emigration from his land of birth, permitted and arranged by God, and made by Him successful through re-establishment in the new land, were links in a nexus of purposes leading to his new assignment as "caller to God." . . . Hasn't God sent him to his new *Medina* that he may freely call the people to the truth? that he may by his eloquence, his "bon example" and his "greater jihad" convince mankind of the truth that God is God . . . ?[21]

Here we see a Muslim form of the "Manifest Destiny" that so shaped our own American heritage. Within an alien environment Islam has established a new beachhead. The Muslim presence is to be something that gradually permeates society and ideally leads increasing numbers of people to the true religion until the whole nation turns.

This spirit participates in the worldwide resurgence that Islam is experiencing, from the renewal brought to Islam by the Muslim Brotherhood[22] and the Islamic Movement,[23] to the Iranian revolution of 1979, and in general as a result of the vast new wealth so many Islamic states have found in oil. Numerous Muslim organizations of North America have been influenced by this spirit. Among these is the Chicago-headquartered Islamic Information Center of America, founded and currently directed by Musa Qutub, a professor of geography. Its objective is "to deliver the Message of Islam in its totality and purity to the American people, to inform non-Muslims about Islam and to aid Americans who embrace Islam in delivering the Message to others."[24] Another is the dynamic Muslim Student Association founded in 1963, with several hundred student chapters around the country. "The most important task which only the MSA can do efficiently," it informs its membership, "is da'wah among non-Muslims."[25] It can do so because of its presence on numerous campuses, places where people are "curious," "inquisitive," and "open-minded." So many groups of nonstudent Muslims affiliated with it that an umbrella organization, the Islamic Society of North America, was established in 1983. This society reaches out both through its publishing arm (North American Islamic Trust, one of many similar Muslim publishing outlets) and its training arm (The Islamic Teaching Center), which prepares young Muslims to be effective bearers of the Muslim message. One notable work has been its outreach perhaps by now to thousands of inmates in hundreds of prisons throughout the United States through correspondence courses. Also important is the Muslim World League founded by the Saudi Arabian government in 1962. It supports outreach throughout the world, including North America. Shi'ites and Ahmadiyya Muslims also have their outreach organizations, the latter having, among other things, a Missionary

Training College in Pakistan. Finally, outreach is integral to the largely African American Muslim groups. Whatever the means, the ultimate goal of these groups is to pervade America with Islamic values and to win converts to Islam by their lives and example.


## NOTES

1. See John O. Voll's use of these categories in "Islamic Issues for Muslims in the United States," in *The Muslims of America*, ed. Yvonne Y. Haddad (New York: Oxford University Press, 1991), 205 and throughout.

2. Cited in Earle Waugh, "Muslim Leadership and the Shaping of the Umma: Classical Tradition and Religious Tension in the North American Setting," in *The Muslim Community in North America*, ed. Earle H. Waugh et al. (Edmonton: University of Alberta Press, 1983), 28; from K. Bagnell, "The Faith of Our Fathers," *The Review* 64:6 (1980): 5.

3. For example, on the matter of taking American names, see Emily Kalled Lovell, "Islam in the United States: Past and Present," in *The Muslim Community*, 100. Other trends toward assimilation include taking on patterns of Protestant denominations, female attendance at prayer services, consumption of alcohol, and social events at mosque basements that include dancing.

4. I borrow the term "mosque community" from Earle Waugh, though I use it in a looser sense than he seems to. Note his comments on Muslim social cohesion and its roots in the old millet system; "Muslim Leadership and the Shaping of the Umma," 22ff. Actually the term "mosque" can mean different things; it can simply designate a group of people who gather for worship, or a building used exclusively for worship, or a structure that shows distinctive Islamic architecture with a minaret or dome. See Yvonne Y. Haddad and Adair T. Lummis, *Islamic Values in the United States* (New York: Oxford University Press, 1987), 35.

5. Detroit Muslims purchased a hall to use for meetings and in 1919 began what was probably the first mosque in the United States. It was later converted into use as a church, however. See Lovell, "Islam in the United States," 101. The worship place (mosque) of the Syrian and Lebanese community in Ross, North Dakota, is sometimes cited as the first U.S. mosque; it was established in 1929. It was recently bulldozed. See Richard Bernstein, "A Growing Islamic Presence: Balancing Sacred and Secular," part 1 of "Muslims in America," *New York Times* (2 May 1993), A-15.

6. The illustrated booklet *Fifty Years of Islam in Iowa 1925–1975* tells about Iowa Muslims (publisher not known).

7. For more detail see Allen E. Richardson, *Islamic Churches in North America: Patterns of Belief and Devotion of Muslims from Asian Countries in the United States and Canada* (New York: Pilgrim Press, 1981), 26–27.

8. See Don Terry, "Black Muslims Enter Islamic Mainstream," part 2 of "Muslims in America," *New York Times* (3 May 1993), A-9.

9. On the 1987 figures see Haddad and Lummis, *Islamic Values in the United States*, 3–4. On the 1993 figures see Richard Bernstein, "A Growing Islamic Presence: Balancing Sacred and Secular," A-1.

10. Compare Haddad and Lummis, *Islamic Values in the United States*, 35.

11. Waugh, "Muslim Leadership and the Shaping of the Umma," 20.

12. On the changing role of the imam, see Earle H. Waugh, "Imam in the New World: Models and Modifications," in *Transitions and Transformations in the History of Religions*, ed. Frank E. Reynolds and Theodore M. Ludwig (Leiden: E. J. Brill, 1980), 124–49.

13. Peter Steinfels, "Despite Role on World Stage, Muslims Turn to the Personal," *New York Times* (7 May 1993), A-13.

14. Robert Franklin, "Pan Am refused to fly Iraqi native home to state," Minneapolis: *Star Tribune* (30 January 1991), A-12. Cited in David D. Grafton, "Muslims as a Minority: Parameters for Encounter and Implications for Lutheran/Muslim Conversation in the Twin Cities," St. Paul: Luther Northwestern Theological Seminary, unpublished paper (1993), 19.

15. See Farar Gilanshah, "Iranians of the Twin Cities," Ph.D. diss. University of Minnesota, Minneapolis (1983), 260. Cited in Grafton, "Muslims as a Minority," 20. See Grafton's general discussion of Muslim political participation in the Twin Cities, pp. 19–25.

16. Steinfels, "Despite Role on World Stage, Muslims Turn to the Personal."

17. While Warith Deen Muhammad does not speak politically for the African American Muslim community, his own views are instructive. *The New York Times* reports: "Last year [1992], he became the first imam ever to give the invocation before the United States Senate. Throughout the 1980s, he voted Republican in Presidential elections because of his own anti-welfare beliefs, and last year he backed President George Bush over Bill Clinton." Don Terry, "Black Muslims Enter Islamic Mainstream."

18. Steinfels, "Despite Role on World Stage, Muslims Turn to the Personal."

19. In the Qur'an, Sura 16.125, we read: "Invite (all) to the Way of thy Lord with wisdom and beautiful preaching; and argue with them in ways that are best and most gracious."

20. Compare Larry Allan Poston's outline of the Muslim Brotherhood's agenda and his contrast between the internal/personal and external/institutional approaches. "Da'wa in the West," in *The Muslims of America*,

ed. Yvonne Yazbeck Haddad (New York: Oxford University Press, 1991), 126ff.

21. Ism'ail R. Al-Faruqi, "Islamic Ideals in North America," in *The Muslim Community*, 268–69.

22. Al-Ikhwan al-Muslimun, founded in 1928 by the Egyptian Hassan al-Banna (1906–1949).

23. Jama'at-i Islami, founded in 1941 by the Indian Abu ala Mawdudi (1903–1979).

24. Larry Allan Poston in Haddad, *The Muslims of America*, 131.

25. Ibid., 132.

# 10

# Relations with the Christian Community

A guide to help Muslim parents as they raise their children in a secular North American society, *Parents' Manual: A Guide for Muslim Parents Living in North America,* gives the encouragement that Muslim children "associate with non-Muslim children in whose homes religious values and high standards of behavior are respected and maintained."[1] This is truly wise guidance. From the outset, it is important to sense how much Muslims and Christians share in their deepest concerns. For both Muslim and Christian, the deepest commitment is to the one and only God who is of infinite mercy. For both, the deepest desire is to live in the will of that one God so that all peoples might know God. "Show us the straight way,"[2] the Muslim daily prays; "Thy kingdom come, thy will be done," the Christian daily prays. This commitment takes concrete shape in our homes as our children are nurtured in it. Together with the Jews, in an important sense parents of us all, we are of Abraham's faith.

This commonality has not hindered Muslims and Christians from fighting and hating each other over the centuries. But today, as these two largest and most dynamic of all the world's religious faiths stand eyeball to eyeball almost everywhere, including the North American setting, it may be the time to seek a reversal of history's precedent; at least we may seek this in North America.

But for that to happen, enormous mountains of misunderstanding must be worked through. Events in recent years do not seem to encourage this "working through"—the rise of OPEC and with it the acknowledged presence of Muslim power in the world, the Iran hostage crisis, the bombing of the marine base in Lebanon, hostages, hijackings, the continued displacement of Palestinians, the death threat to Salman Rushdie, the Persian Gulf War, the rape of Bosnia, the bombing of the New York World Trade Center . . . this list will not stop soon.

These mountains of hatred and ill will can begin to dissipate only as people of goodwill on each side make the appropriate effort. Certainly North America is an ideal location for this process to begin, a place to which countless Muslims have freely chosen to emigrate, to work and to raise their families.

So let us return to the admonition to devout Muslim parents that their children be encouraged to make friends with children of devout Christian families rather than of families with no Christian principles. Let us assume this counsel as the climate for pondering our mutual relationships.


## HOME AND FAMILY

There are at least three arenas in which our mutual relations are forged. The first is our most intimate field of relationships, the home and family life amid neighbors and community. The parents' manual to which I referred above deals with this arena as the Muslim experiences it. Perhaps, in fact, the most immediate contact many of our families will have with the Muslim is through our children. Can friendships here be fostered? Might not the close-knit character of the devout Muslim family help to strengthen our own need for well-knit, healthy families? If there are Muslim families in our neighborhood, we will welcome them to be a contributing part of the larger community life. And as this happens we will be alert to issues that may create difficulties for such families: different standards in boy-girl relationships that may affect the degree to which Muslim children may feel free to participate in school sports or school-related entertainment; or food and dietary concerns; or difficulties they may experience with our festivals even as their own festivals are ignored by society generally.

The local mosque or Islamic center may invite community participation on certain occasions. Such times present an opportunity for a larger acquaintance. Our churches can reciprocate, or initiate family get-togethers between mosqued and churched people. Such occasions can create the environment for coming to know each other and sharing each other's joys and concerns. If, on the other hand, the Muslim family fails to experience hospitality at this most basic level, it will forge not a sense of welcome but of isolation, generating its own set of dynamics. It is at this level, of the most intimate circle of relationships, that Muslim families often experience the greatest difficulty within North American society.

Conformity of Christians to passing cultural norms may be one of the weakest links in our Christian witness. Muslim youth, as do many Christian youth, often drift away from their heritage and appropriate without qualms the surrounding cultural values. There are accounts of such alienated Muslim youth returning to their faith, or of nominal Christians converting to an active Muslim faith. Typical of their witness is that of Ms. Lahaj, a third-generation member of a Lebanese family. A child of the 1960s, and a folk singer and writer in Greenwich Village in the 1970s, she says, "[I] reached a point where I felt spiritually bankrupt." Eventually, after years of searching, she rediscovered Islam. "When I embraced Islam," she said, "I felt like I was embracing something that hadn't been tainted by our culture, everything there had been the same for 1,400 years. I was looking for purpose and structure and meaning, and I found it."[3]


## ECONOMIC AND PROFESSIONAL RELATIONSHIPS

A second arena within which relationships are forged is the wider world of economic and professional activities. Opportunities in this arena are, in fact, among the principal factors that draw Muslims to these shores. Muslims of North America are the most highly educated and professionalized Muslim population in the world. This is very different from, say, the European Muslim population, for which labor opportunities have been a primary drawing card. By and large this economic and professional arena offers Muslims wide and generally unbiased opportunities. Nevertheless, difficulties might be encountered in the workplace, such as respect for the Muslim's day of worship (Friday), accommodation during the month of fasting (Ramadan), and recognition of Muslim festival days. In this world of business, too, the use of money becomes a critical factor, one that may even affect the Muslim at the family level—the purchase of a home, for instance. Devout Muslims will often be unable to negotiate contracts based on borrowing money at interest. How then can they purchase homes and property?

In one city, the Muslim community wished to buy a piece of school property, costing perhaps around half a million dollars, for its Islamic center. After an initial fruitless conversation with bank officials, with whom they sought to borrow money on some basis other than interest, they shared their problem with their lawyer. "Well," he said, "let me see if I can help you." Some days later he called the local Muslim leaders and informed them that some of his friends were willing to put up the needed money without interest. "There is only one problem," he said. "These friends of mine are Jewish. Will that be a problem for you?" "Not at all," the Muslims replied. And so the Jewish community enabled the Muslim community to purchase property for its Islamic center.

## RECOGNITION AND JUSTICE

The day for a higher public profile of Muslims in political life is perhaps still some way off, though beginnings have been made. As do others within American society, Muslims seek for greater justice, the third arena in which mutual relations are forged. One institution in which progress has been made is the military. During World War II a young Muslim officer, Abdallah Igram from Cedar

Rapids, Iowa, discovered that his religious classification was "X," since he did not fit the categories of Protestant, Catholic, or Jew. Subsequently, in an effort to remedy this lack of recognition of Muslims in the United States society generally, he inspired some four hundred Muslims to gather and form the International Muslim Society, later to be called the Federation, in Cedar Rapids in June 1952.[4]

Another institution within which greater justice is sought is the judicial and prison system. Although the courts have defined Islam as a religion, both on the basis of the "theism" and "ultimate concern" criteria, religious rights for Muslim prisoners have not been automatic. More than one prison riot has had treatment of Muslims as one of its ingredients.[5] Only through court cases have First Amendment rights been extended to such persons so that they "have the right to assemble for religious services, to consult a cleric of their faith, to possess religious publications and subscribe to religious literature, to wear unobtrusive religious symbols such as medallions, to have prepared a special diet required by their religion, and to correspond with their spiritual leaders."[6]

## THE ROLE OF THE CHURCH

Related to all three arenas is the church. How does or how ought the church relate to Muslim interests or needs in these various arenas? In its local expression, as well as at the national level, and all the way in between, the church will relate to the Muslim community in North America in particular and various ways.

Just as a wide range of Muslim attitudes shape Muslims' understanding of their relations with Christians,[7] so also is it the case with Christians. One might envision these attitudes falling somewhere amid three points on a triangle, these three points representing (1) avoidance or fear; (2) conversionist attitudes; and (3) a dialogical orientation. Perhaps at the present time avoidance or fear is the prevailing mood among many within the churches. Others, however, particularly within Christian fundamentalist groups, are strongly conversionist in their attitude, seeking in every way to humiliate the Muslim and proclaim the superiority of Christianity, using a good dose of polemics (spoken or written) in the process. Yet others are dialogical, most notably the ecumenically minded churches, seeing the goal of relationship as being that of under-standing and tolerance.

Where ought we to fall amid these three points? Perhaps we need to construct a new triangle, one that replaces fear with respect, maintains a genuine dialogue for the sake of mutual understanding and comprehension, while enlivened at the same time by an evan-gelical concern that faithful witness be borne to the gospel of God's love in Jesus Christ.

We might consider national organizations in this light. Or-ganizations that work within the framework of the World Council of Churches' understanding of dialogue[8] include the Duncan Black Macdonald Center for the Study of Islam and Christian-Muslim Relations, located at Hartford Seminary, founded in 1975; the Office of Christian-Muslim Concerns of the National Council of Christian Churches in the USA, established in 1977, located at the above center; and the Interfaith Office of the Presbyterian Church (USA), established a decade later. The primary concerns of these organi-zations are relations of mutual respect and understanding among Muslims and Christians in North America, interaction through di-alogue, representation on each other's councils where mutual in-terests are at stake, and common action for social justice. With similar concerns, but working within the framework of the Second Vatican Council,[9] the Secretariat for Ecumenical and Interreligious Affairs was established in 1987 by the National Conference of Catholic Bishops.

Other organizations established in recent years give a more explicit place to the evangelical intent of inviting the Muslim to faith in Jesus Christ; for instance, the Department of Interfaith Witness under the Home Mission Board of the Southern Baptist Convention. Their booklet, *Beliefs of Other Kinds: A Guide to Interfaith Witness in the United States*, and the more recently published *Meeting the World: Ministering Cross-Culturally*,[10] both of which have chapters on Islam, set forth the governing perspective. The Zwemer Institute of Islamic Studies takes an aggressive conversionist stance toward

Muslims generally. Other somewhat more ephemeral groups, such as the "Fellowship of Isa (Jesus),"[11] introduce a strongly polemical element into the relationship with Muslims. Even as late as 1978, the Zwemer Institute published a keynote address by Stanley Mooneyham that spoke of "the defensive reaction engineered by Satan as he sees his Islamic stronghold threatened."[12]

Reformed and Lutheran groups have attempted to be explicit, perhaps not yet entirely successfully, about the double dimensions of dialogue and proclamation. In a cautiously worded statement, the Reformed Church of America rejects "Muslim-as-convert" as a necessary corollary of dialogue and cooperation with the Muslim. But it also speaks of the individual Christian as "Christ-in-the-flesh," a bold statement to be sure. In cumbersome language, perhaps reflecting some lack of decisiveness, it suggests that somehow when Muslims "avail themselves of the Christian offering and receive the Christian into their hearts as friend," they "receive Christ and avail themselves of him. They eat and drink of that friendship and, through the faithfulness of their Christian friends, Christ is remembered in them."[13]

A Lutheran document is somewhat less tortured in its language. This document, which reflects theologically on the relationship between Muslims and Christians, in the concluding pages responds to the question, "Frankly, I guess what I want to know is whether you want us to make disciples of Muslim peoples." The answer given by the director of the Division for World Mission and Interchurch Cooperation reads:

> If you mean do you want the hearts and minds of our Muslim friends to be captured and molded by God who raised Jesus from the dead, then I desire that they be disciples! If you mean do you want Muslim people to find faith, hope, and love in God's incredible prophetic embodiment in Jesus, then I desire that they know and live within this truth! If you mean do you want them to be participants within a community of faith who, through the power of the God embodied in Jesus, live out their lives in mutual confession, affirmation, and mission, then I would hope that this could be a living reality for them. . . . However, if you mean do I insist that life and salvation can only be found in *membership* in our Christian . . . churches, then I know that the traditional social structures of Islamic society, the

historical tensions existing between our communities and the brokenness of our own Christian churches may make that an impos-
sibility. It may mean that God intends to work out God's own future
for Christians and Muslims in terms that we have not dreamed of.[14]

Besides these and other national organizations, numerous
initiatives in cities with significant Muslim populations have led to
the formation of interfaith councils and other forms of interfaith
cooperation and activity. One such example was the significant
conference held in Chicago in April 1993 sponsored by the Association of Chicago Theological Schools on "Christian-Muslim Relations: Towards a Just World Order." Christians will want to be
alert to such events.

In the final analysis, the greatest opportunities for relating in
a Christianly way with Muslims lie in the local setting. Christians
have the opportunity to be good neighbors to Muslims. Christians
can be supportive of Muslim neighbors in their needs and alert to
the ways our society offends and isolates them. In the context of
friendship, as we ask about their faith, they will ask about ours,
and the opportune moment for testimony to God's love in Christ
will be there. It is in this living contact that we will learn genuine
appreciation of each other, will discover the concrete meaning of
mutual service, will become teachers to each other, and will at the
same time, in fact, bear the most effective and enduring witness
to Jesus Christ.

## NOTES

1. The Women's Committee of the MSA, *Parents' Manual: A Guide for
Muslim Parents Living in North America* (Brentwood, Md.: American Trust
Publications, 1976), 21.

2. Sura 1.6.

3. For a fuller account of her reconversion, as well as that of others,
see Ari L. Goldman, "Mosque's New Era: Growth and Good Will," in Elias
D. Mallon ed., *Neighbors: Muslims in North America* (New York: Friendship
Press, 1989), 4–12.

4. Emily Kalled Lovell, "Islam in the United States: Past and Present,"
in *The Muslim Community in North America*, ed. Earle H. Waugh et al.
(Edmonton: University of Alberta Press, 1983), 104.

5. A recent example was an uprising in a correctional facility in Lucasville, Ohio. The grievances included "religious oppression of Muslims" that "prevented them from practicing their religion as they saw fit, for instance by denying them prayer beads, prayer oils and traditional clothing." The black guard who had been taken hostage said he had undergone a conversion to Islam in the process. See Ronald Smothers, "Second Hostage Is Freed Unhurt by Ohio Inmates," *New York Times* (17 April 1993), 6.

6. Kathleen Moore, "Muslims in Prison: Claims to Constitutional Protection of Religious Liberty," in *The Muslims of America*, ed. Yvonne Y. Haddad (New York: Oxford University Press, 1991), 139.

7. Yvonne Y. Haddad and Adair T. Lummis identify five prevailing worldviews among immigrant Muslims in America: (1) liberal, the most Americanized segment and without explicit organizational form; (2) conservative, Westernized but adhering to minimal Muslim requirements in piety and diet; (3) evangelical, placing strong emphasis on the normative role of scripture and sunna or example of the prophet and detailed attention to Islamic prescriptions for life, tending to emphasize cohesion of devout Muslims, often inviting itinerant Muslim missionaries to lecture on faithfulness to Islam, even from time to time reaching out to a wider public and to churches through lecture bureaus and dialogue events; (4) neonormative, similar to the former but including commitment to the importance of public supervision of life by Islam, involving thereby questions of state; and (5) Sufis, mystics focusing on inwardness. Perhaps to these should be added the extremist or radical, who is willing to use force for the sake of Islam. *Islamic Values in the United States* (New York: Oxford University Press, 1987), 170–71.

8. See *Guidelines on Dialogue with People of Living Faiths and Ideologies* (Geneva: World Council of Churches, 1979).

9. See "Declaration on the Relationship of the Church to Non-Christian Religions," in *The Documents of Vatican II: With Notes and Comments by Catholic, Protestant, and Orthodox Authorities*, ed. Walter M. Abbott and Joseph Gallagher (New York: Guild Press, 1966), 660–68. See also the publication of the Secretariat for Non-Christian Religions, *Guidelines for a Dialogue Between Muslims and Christians* (Rome: Libreria Editrice Ancora, 1969). It has been noted that the guidelines document is "the first book of its kind by any Christian organization"; Byron L. Haines, "Perspectives of American Churches on Islam and the Muslim Community in America; An Analysis of Some Official and Unofficial Statements," in *The Muslims of America*, 49 n. 10.

10. New Hope, P.O. Box 12065, Birmingham, Ala., 1992.

11. Their literature gives their address as P.O. Box 35471, Minneapolis, Minn. 55435.

12. W. Stanley Mooneyham, "Keynote Address," in *The Gospel and Islam: A 1978 Compendium*, ed. Don M. McCurry (Monrovia, Calif.: Missions Advanced Research and Communications Center, 1979), 23–24. The volume as a whole presents a variety of views, some being much more respectful and dialogical in nature.

13. See "The Muslim Community in a Christian Perspective," in *Perspectives* (January 1987): 8–11. For a clearer and helpful reflection from a similar Presbyterian perspective, see Byron L. Haines and Frank L. Cooley, eds., *Christians and Muslims Together: An Exploration by Presbyterians* (Philadelphia: Geneva Press, 1987).

14. *God and Jesus: Theological Reflections for Christian-Muslim Dialog* (Minneapolis: Division for World Mission and Interchurch Cooperation/ The American Lutheran Church, 1986), 93–94. This division has been superceded by the Division for Global Mission of the Evangelical Lutheran Church in America.

# PART THREE

# Islam—Movements and Emphases

PILGRIMS CAMPING OUTSIDE MECCA

# 11

## The Shi'ites

Strictly speaking, faith in the one God and in Muhammad as the last in a line of prophets from God is the only required faith statement in Islam. The vast majority of Muslims known as the Sunnis as well as the Shi'ites rely on the same confession: "I confess that there is no God but Allah, and Muhammad is his prophet!"

All Muslims believe that the Qur'an is the final revelation from God. Sunnis and Shi'ites are no different in their piety, its public practice in prayer, rituals, commandments, and prohibitions. The differences between Shi'ites and Sunnis relate to the leadership in Islam, in the interpretation of the Qur'an, and in legal decisions.

### THE ORIGIN OF THE SHI'ITES

The Shi'ites, or Shia, originated in an argument within Islam about who should be the legitimate successor to Muhammad after his death in 632. The majority of influential Muslims, later known as Sunnis, agreed to name a caliph (successor) who could unite the religious and political leadership of Muslims in one person, but could in no respect claim divine legitimate authority.

A minority of Muslims disagreed with this decision. They were convinced that God himself would determine Muhammad's successors and that Muhammad's successor must come from his family.

That is why they believed they had found the caliph chosen by God in Ali, the cousin and son-in-law of Muhammad. Because these Muslims believed Ali to be the first rightful successor, they were called *shi'at Ali*, "of Ali's party," by the Sunnis.

Ali could only briefly carry out the caliphate, which was then recognized by all Muslims, because he was murdered in 661 after only five years of service. His sons Hasan and Husayn could not succeed him because the powerful ruler of Damascus took over the caliphate and then bound the position by decree to his own dynasty.

The murder of Husayn in 680 brought about the final separation of the Shi'ites from the rest of the Islamic leadership. Shi'ites today still commemorate Husayn's death date, the tenth day of the month Muharram, with processions and passion plays of both martyrs, Husayn and Ali. Many Shi'ites make a pilgrimage on this day to Husayn's grave site in Kerbala in Iraq. The pilgrims try to relive the martyrdoms of Ali and Husayn. This ritual includes sacrificial songs and self-castigation to the point of bodily harm—pounding on the breast with chains and swords.

## THE IMAM

All Muslims use the title *imam* for the person leading prayer in the mosque; in Arabic *amam* means "in front." For Shi'ites, however, this title has an additional meaning: *Imam* for them designates the single, legitimate leader of Islam, who is descended from Muhammad's family. Thus the title is sometimes seen as a spiritual cloak that can be passed from one wearer to another, but at the same time exists eternally independent of a human wearer. This understanding has far-reaching consequences, particularly in legal questions and in respect to expectations of the "last things."

Shi'ites believe that the Imam is appointed by God and therefore shares in divine knowledge. He makes the decisive interpretation of religious and secular laws. Even the Qur'an is perfected only through his interpretation. The Imam fights injustice and restores justice where it has been violated. The Imam and his representatives have great influence over the life of the individual and the shape of society and thus also have political power. Although he is named by humans, his election is predetermined by God. He serves as the living carrier of God's law, commissioned by God, and is therefore seen as sinless.

For most Shi'ites the succession of Imams in a straight dynastic line was decisive. When this line was first interrupted and then completely broken, they put their hopes in the *Mahdi,* "the true guide," the coming savior.

This hope joined the idea of the *ghaybah,* the hiding of the Imam: The last legitimate Imam has been taken into eternity and will return at the end of time as the Imam Mahdi. From his hiding, the Imam was able to continue to exert his spiritual influence. Thus the leader and ruler of the Shi'ites has only the role of "governor" until the return of the Mahdi or Imam.

In the absence of the Imam, the *mujtahidun,* the legal scholars, are the only ones able to correctly interpret Qur'anic law. In addition, the Shi'ites see in these scholars the authority of the Qur'an. This attitude allows Shi'ites a very flexible interpretation of the strict laws in the Qur'an; it takes into account historical and societal changes. Thus the interpretation and application of laws can be modified and enhanced from case to case. By contrast, the Sunnis' tendency to solidify the laws and their interpretation can make needed change difficult.

Especially important in the history of Shi'ites is their experience of opposition to various Sunni rulers. The feelings of betrayal, of suffering, and of courage to resist characterize their entire lives and color their piety. This is noticeable, for example, in their attachment to personalities and their veneration of the saints.

## SHI'ITE GROUPS

Through the notion of an Imam who is hidden and will come again, the Shi'ites became increasingly characterized by this hope and expectation of his return. And yet various Shi'ite branches arose with differing leadership structures.

One group is led by the *da'i*, the proclaimer of the eternal Imam, the others (the Twelvers) by the *ayat allahs* (Ayatollahs), "the signs of God," or representatives of the Imam. *Ayatollah* was at first a title of honor given by the Twelvers to significant Muslims because of their authority and power to inspire. Some Shi'ites saw their task as establishing political leadership, others worked on contemporary interpretation of law and the care of the Shi'ite community. But all understood themselves to be messengers of the Imam to come again.

All Shi'ites held strictly to the dynastic succession of Imams, but by 740 disagreements had arisen. The Zaidites developed new concepts of leadership completely different from the prior understanding. They looked for the Imam among the many descendants of Ali, that is, of his sons. The requirements for appointment to serve as Imam were: following God's path, normal intellectual abilities, and courage. Sometimes the Zaidites had several Imams simultaneously. Although the Zaidites continued the argument with the Sunni leadership, they did recognize the first Sunni caliph (before Ali) and followed Sunni teachings for the most part. To this day the Zaidites exert great influence in North Yemen on religious and political questions.

A further split arose when the sixth Imam, Jafar as-Sudik, did not name his eldest son, Ismail, to be the next Imam, but a younger son. Some Shi'ites still recognized Ismail as the legitimate seventh Imam; therefore they are called Ismailis or Seveners. Ismail disappeared in the middle of the eighth century, and he is awaited by Ismailites as the Mahdi to come again. The Ismailites succeeded in organizing themselves into units that mostly work underground. In the tenth century they were able to raise up the Fatimid Empire in Egypt. Today the Ismailites are a small minority; spread out all over the world, they live mostly as wealthy merchants with a distinct sense of community. Their chief calls himself Aga Khan.

The *ithna Ashariyah*, or "Twelvers," form another group among the Imami-Shi'ites, that is, followers of the Shi'ite Imam tradition. They recognize twelve Imams and assume that the twelfth Imam went to "the great concealment" in 940 according to our calendar. The Twelver Shi'ites were persecuted many times by the Sunnis and the majority of them were pushed into Iraq and Iran. This Shi'ite branch became the state religion of Persia in 1501 and was declared the foundation of the Islamic Republic of Iran after the revolution of 1979. Leadership of the Twelver Shi'ites at present is controlled by more than seventy Ayatollahs. The Ayatollah Khomeini, the Ayatollah of the holy city of Ghom, was among this group.

## SHI'ITES TODAY

It is difficult to determine the total number of Shi'ites, of whom many live in countries with Sunni majorities. Probably about one-tenth of all Muslims belong to the Shi'ites. In addition, other small subgroups exist:

- The Nusayriyah or Alawites, a group in Syria and South Anatolia often called ultra-Shi'ite, who venerate Ali as almost divine.
- The Druze in Lebanon, Syria, and Israel, organized primarily in "secret societies."
- The Batinis in Iraq, who have developed an appreciation of Western scientific thinking.
- The Ali Ilahis in Iran and Turkestan (formerly part of the USSR), who honor Ali as God.
- The Bektashi in Turkey and Albania, oriented toward mysticism.

# 12

## Mysticism and Sufism

### THE WAY OF LOVE TO GOD

About 150 years after Muhammad's death, a simply dressed woman in Basra, a port city in Iraq, aroused a sensation. She ran through the alleys of the city with a burning torch in one hand and a bucket of water in the other: "I want to catch paradise on fire and pour water on hell so that the veils disappear and it becomes clear who is praying to God out of love, and not out of fear of hell or hope for paradise." Rabiah al-Adawiyah (d. 801) was seen as a "second Mary," as a saint (*wali*). She belonged to the Sufis, who dress in wool (*suf*) and strive for purity before God.

Prior to this it was not love, but fear of God and the last judgment, that motivated ascetics like Hasan al-Basri (d. 728) and his students. They protested—like the Christian desert monks—against luxury and the superficiality of society, and called people to return to God. This movement gained a deeper dimension through Rabiah, the onetime slave: Whoever truly believes loves God. Only those who love God can experience his closeness; for lovers direct all their actions and thoughts toward their beloved— toward God, in order to be with him like a drop of water in the ocean.

Sufism is the Islamic form of mysticism, focused on internalizing faith. It sees itself as the direct "message of the heart." Mystics see their entire lives as a path (*tariqah*) to union with God.


## THE WAY—IN THE QUR'AN AND ACCORDING TO MUHAMMAD

Mystics find their way already prescribed in the Qur'an; for example, in the challenge to turn away from those who do not think about God and follow his guidance (Sura 53.29). For Sufis, words like "and seek of the Bounty of Allah: and celebrate the Praises of Allah often (and without stint)" (Sura 62.10) and "Allah loves those who do good to others" (*al-muhsinin*—compare Sura 5.93) have become essential words for the way, at the end of which stands the experience of God's truth. Whoever follows this path will receive God's signs, which only those who are faithful can understand (Sura 51.20).

The mystics believe they can find directions for their path in Muhammad. Thus the Persian Salman, who was influenced by pre-Islamic mystical currents in Iran, belonged to the prophet's most intimate circle. This gave legitimacy to his mystical orientation. Mystics also refer to the fact that Muhammad taught the remembrance of God (*dhikr*) to Abu Bakr, later the first caliph, in a cave during the Hijra in the most dangerous hours of the flight to Medina.

But above all, Muhammad himself had miraculous experiences in the night of his journey to Jerusalem and then his ascension to heaven (Sura 17.1). With this background, he shared guidance in a language of experience and love and spoke of the renewal of God's covenant with all souls. Sufis recognize Muhammad as the "perfect human" guided by God, diverted by no human teachings, a "friend of God," on the right path to God. With this in mind, every founder and leader of Sufi orders deems it important that he stand in Muhammad's tradition in this special way.

## MARTYRS AND TEACHERS

Sufis tried to find the deeper, hidden meaning of the Qur'an's words and to internalize the apparently external rules for living. Thus they fulfilled the longing of many people. Some earned great respect, while others suffered hatred and enmity.

Al-Hallaj, Husayn ibn Mansur, for example, died in 922 in Baghdad on a cross—and became for the mystics a "martyr of God's love." He had grown up during the slave rebellions in Iraq and could not stop his search for God. It became clear to him that the divine truth "hides from discovery and is too holy to be seen with the eye." Still he later witnessed, "I saw my Lord with my heart's eye and said, 'Who are you?' He answered, 'You.' " In ecstasy he cried out, "*Ana al-Haqq*—I am the Truth." His opponents translated, "I am the true one (= God)." They accused him of exceeding the boundaries between God and humans. In addition, Al-Hallaj also called for social changes. Doing so cost him his life.

Abu Hamid Muhammad al-Ghazzali (1058–1111) had a very different experience. While the West was arming itself for the crusades, he lived out a shining scholarly career in Baghdad. He became a wandering Sufi, a dervish. The limits of logical thinking had become clear to him. But even as a mystic, he did not want to actually merge with God in ecstasy. In his all-loving approach, he knew he had to submit himself to God's will. Al-Ghazzali became one of the greatest teachers of Sunni Islam. His writings still give people direction. Because of the expansiveness of his thinking, as well as his tolerance toward Jews and Christians, his influence has reached far beyond the "house of Islam." Thomas Aquinas studied his writings as did the Christian mystic Meister Eckhart. Al-Ghazzali died with the words, "I hear and belong: Onward to the entrance to the king."

## THE ORDERS

A new phase began for the mystical movement with the foundation
of the Qadariyah order in 1135. More and more students followed
respected Sufi masters to form fraternities and formal orders.
"Cloisters" (*zawiya*, literally "corner") are spiritual and intellectual
centers in which new arrivals are often led through months-long
training, and accepted members find refuge and regularly gather
for community days. Ascetic cloister life and celibacy are foreign
to Islam; the members of the orders by contrast are to act as models
in everyday life. These mystic communities are well entrenched in
the life of Islamic countries. The main orders have branches from
Indonesia to Morocco; others are limited by region.

In the life of the orders, besides the founders there are successors, called *sheiks* (shaykhs) or *pirs*, and their representatives
(caliphs). Beginners are "students" (*murid*) before these leaders as
well as before all members of the order. In absolute obedience the
student gives his very self to the sheik, then to the founder, then
to Muhammad, so as to finally "lose" himself (*fana*, literally "ex-
tinction") in God. But a just spiritual master does not bind his
followers to himself. He is no mediator between the student and
God, but a co-traveler on the common way—even if a few steps
ahead. The master wants to free his student from love of the world
and release him from all arrogance. All mere appearance of holiness
and status-seeking should be overcome, just as should envy, wrath,
sensuousness, and greed for material things and worldly recognition. Only in this way can the striving grow in the heart to be
completely absorbed in God. Therefore the roots binding a person's
own soul (*an-nafs al-ammarah*; literally "soul that inclines to evil")
to the world must be torn out in the struggle with the self. This is
the *jihad akbar*, the "great war" (effort).

## CONSTANT REMEMBRANCE OF
## GOD (*DHIKR*)

The source of power in the mystical path is the constant remembrance of God, *dhikr*.

Every Muslim practices *dhikr* in traditional prayer. But the mystic goes beyond the fulfillment of duty (Sura 29.45). *Dhikr* is to encompass the entire life. In remembering and glorifying God's name (Sura 73.8; 76.25) the lover joins in with the songs of praise and the God-remembrance of the entire earthly and heavenly creation, inaudible to humans. This happens immediately following the traditional prayer with the help of the *mishaba*, the "rose wreath," when the person praying recites the short statements of praise to God thirty-three times in accordance with the number of prayer beads: *subhan Allah*, "Glory be to Allah"; *al-hamdala-Llah*, "Praise be to Allah"; *Allahu akbar*, "Allah is greater"; or when he or she contemplates the ninety-nine names of God. When this thought about God includes the confession *la ilaha illa-Llah*, "There is no God but Allah," then the following is promised: When seven heavens and their inhabitants and seven earths are put onto a scale and this statement on the other side, these words are weightier at the judgment.

Many Muslims carry out a "silent *dhikr*." Unnoticed in their environment, they concentrate in the midst of a workday on God-remembrance so that they can direct all their actions toward God. This is the essence of *dhikr*, they say.

Beyond this, the Sufi communities are familiar with regularly recurring gatherings for a common *dhikr*, often following a traditional prayer. Despite variations in tradition and method, it includes the recurrence of certain key elements:

- *Ilahis*, songs of glory to God and the prophet Muhammad for bringing the divine light, but also for naming all the prophets, the angels, the saints, and the teachers.
- Qur'an recitations, generally from key portions like the light or throne verse (Sura 24.35-40 and 2.255).
- Innumerable repetitions of one of the names of God or one of the first statements of the confession of faith. The sheik determines the names to be repeated as well as the tempo and rhythm of speaking and breathing. This constantly escalating manner of breathing finally leads to the experience of submission in which all consciousness is eliminated. For example, the first syllable of God's name Allah could be

uttered on inhaling, the second recited with a long exhalation. Other names are often used as well: *rahman* and *rahim*, "the beneficent" and "the merciful"; *hayy*, "the ever-living"; *qayyum*, "self-subsisting"; *rabb*, "Lord"; *ahad*, "the only one"; or the confession statement, *Allah-hu*, "God is HE," the actually inexpressible, all-encompassing, in whom the I of a person finds its goal and end.

Whether a *dhikr* is to be carried out while sitting, standing, or even dancing is determined by the tradition of the particular order. Each movement is given a deeper meaning. The dervishes of the Sufi master Jalal ad-Din ar-Rumi (d. 1272) throw off their black overgarments as symbols of the burden and darkness of the world in order to carry out their round dance in white garments as a symbol of the heavenly world. All the while, they whirl around like butterflies in the sun or as a group around an open center, like heaven and earth around the creator.

## ISLAMIC MYSTICISM IN THE WEST

Since the turn of the twentieth century, Islamic mysticism has gained a strong foothold in the West. Hazrat Inayat Khan from India and his son have sought to develop a "Sufi order of the West," and Idris Sayed Shah develops Sufi understanding and practices in his writings, adapted to the West. In striving for a universal service to God, they try to get behind all dogmas and to transcend the boundaries between religions. Other masters are stricter, saying that all mysticism needs to be directed toward the life and example of Muhammad.

# 13

## Religion, State, Society

### THE IDEAL SOCIETY OF THE
### EARLY PERIOD

Religion and politics, the spiritual and the secular are much more closely related in Islam than they usually are in Christianity. The relationship of the two realms has been described variously in Islam. Contemporary cultural and political differences have played a part. In general the first Muslim community in Medina serves as a paradigm. The Muslims who emigrated from Mecca formed a community (*umma*) with those of Medina. At the beginning a significant Jewish portion of the population was included in spite of religious differences. Arguments, whether of religious or secular nature, were to be brought before "God and Muhammad, his prophet," for Muhammad was recognized as prophet and political leader. The Qur'an expressly demands:

> O ye who believe! Obey Allah, and obey the Messenger, and those charged with authority among you. If ye differ in anything among yourselves, refer it to Allah and His Messenger. (Sura 4.59)

God was recognized as the actual head of the community. At the same time the common advice (*shura*) of the prophet with the Muslims played an important role.

The goal in the giving of advice was to arrive at common, agreed-upon decisions, not to dictate them. This later formed a counterbalance to attempts to erect dictatorships. The modern Islamic understanding of democracy is also connected with this understanding. The Sunnis view the early Islamic period, namely the period of Muhammad and the first four "rightly guided" caliphs, as ideal. Numerous subsequent efforts at reform strive for a return to this ideal.

The caliphs served as Muhammad's successors, although not in his capacity as prophet and bearer of God's revelation. They had the duty to lead the community and protect it, to make its unity apparent, and to protect and enforce divine law within it. The caliphate lost importance in the course of the centuries. The Ottoman sultan took over this position in 1517. The caliphate was eliminated in 1924 under Kamal Ataturk.

Sunni Islam did not form any religious institutions comparable to the church, not even the office of pastor or priest. Even the legal scholars and theologians have no spiritual position in Sunni Islam. The imam is the head of the community, but no intermediary is needed between a person and God.

## ISLAMIC LAW AS THE BASIS FOR COMMUNITY

Islam is a communal and public religion that is all-encompassing, ordering all aspects of life. The "five pillars" themselves, which determine the basic obligations of Muslim life, are public, communal confessions for behavior (see chapters 3 and 4). These can be enhanced by personal piety, but not replaced.

This understanding of religion also characterizes the role of law in Islam. Muslims are addressed in the Qur'an as "the best of Peoples, evolved for mankind, enjoining what is right, forbidding what is wrong, and believing in Allah" (Sura 3.110). Muslims say they are "the best" in that they do these things. A governmental system is therefore only recognized as Islamic if it endorses the obligatory principles written in the Qur'an and the sunna. The sunna, which comprise Muhammad's exemplary actions and sayings, together with the Qur'an, form the basis for Islamic law.

Since the end of colonial control many Islamic countries have tried to assimilate their Western-influenced legal systems and economies into an Islamic framework. Even before this, enduring arrangements of cohabitation between Muslims and non-Muslims have developed outside the framework of an Islamic state in southeastern Europe and parts of Africa, India, and Indonesia. Nevertheless, wherever Muslims are in the minority, such as in Europe or North America, they confront the particular difficulty that Islam in its complete sense cannot be realized since the sharia does not have public validity. Despite this, Muslims living in the West emphasize that they can follow their faith here, too, as long as they are accepted in their uniqueness as equal partners.

## LEGAL STATUS OF NON-MUSLIMS IN THE ISLAMIC STATE

The relationship of Islam to other religious faiths is handled in the Qur'an from a legal perspective. Islam technically allows no place for polytheistic religions in the Islamic community. The practice in fact was often more tolerant. On the other hand, faiths derived from Islam like Baha'i, and groups seen as heretical like the Ahmadiyya, are not tolerated, or only temporarily so, in many Islamic states.

Jews and Christians are considered in the Qur'an to be "people of the book." They are communities (*umma*) to whom God sent revelations in Scripture through a prophet (Moses, Jesus). They really ought to recognize that the earlier revelation issued to them now exists in the Qur'an in perfected form, purified of all distortions. They should not, however, be forced to this recognition. In this regard a short chapter in the Qur'an states:

Say: O ye that reject Faith! I worship not that which ye worship, nor will ye worship that which I worship. . . . To you be your Way, and to me mine. (Sura 109)

The conversion of Muslims to another faith, on the other hand, is decidedly ruled out. To become a Christian is to regress to a lower level of revelation. Yet, various "communities" may live beside one another. Islam has tolerated these "possessors of Scripture" who have closed themselves to the "call (*dawah*) of Islam" as tributary "charges," "protected ones" (*dhimmi*) in its midst, and has given them long-term legal security and protection. From this way of thinking, the Ottoman Empire (Turkey and surroundings) developed a system of non-Islamic communities (*millet*) with limited autonomy. As their charges, the non-Muslims did not have equal rights and ranks, but had to accept numerous disadvantages. The practice of their faith was subject to limitations. Public manifestations of their faith, such as in processions, were forbidden. This is still true in many Islamic countries today. From time to time the Islamic majority did persecute other faiths, but often the motivation was based on other than religious reasons.

## THE SO-CALLED "HOLY WAR" (*JIHAD*)

The Arabic word *jihad*, which is misleadingly translated in the West as "holy war," actually means "great effort," namely effort for the cause of God's will (*jihad fi-sabil Allah*), and can refer to an internal as well as an external struggle. In the centuries after Muhammad, which were distinguished by the spread of war, the "abode of peace" (*dar al-Islam*) was distinguished from the "abode of war" (*dar al-harb*), regions deemed hostile to Islam. In a later period the "abode of treaty" (*dar al-sulh*) became recognized as a region that had not yet achieved full Islamic peace yet was not a region of warfare. The violent defense or spread of Islamic rule was considered by some a special form of *jihad*. Islamic mysticism soon spiritualized the term. The spiritual war was regarded as the "great *jihad*" over the "small *jihad*," the warlike operation. Peaceable efforts, too, such as the effort to achieve just and healthy social conditions, can be termed *jihad*. This concept has been used in the past for efforts to achieve liberation from colonialism, for commitment to the Palestinian cause, and—in Shi'ite Islam—for resistance to the regime of the Shah. The term is often used or misused by militant groups. Generally, every effort to build an Islamic world order, to realize God's revealed will, and to bring his word to power constitutes *jihad*.

The widespread thesis in the West concerning "the spread of Islam by fire and sword" overlooks the difference Muslims perceive between Islamic political jurisdiction and the conversions of individuals to Islam. This thesis likewise overlooks the violent and forceful measures taken by Christians, as in medieval Spain. Wherever Islamic jurisdiction spread violently, the violence was not commited primarily in order to convert people of other faiths. Of course, conversion was promoted by such action. In contrast to this, the expansion of Islam into Africa, Indonesia, and the Philippines was completed for the most part peacefully, especially through trade.

## THE SHI'ITES AND THE IRANIAN REVOLUTION

The Shi'ites in Persia (Iran) usually opposed Sunni control, and thereby suffered persecution. They thereby also developed a spirit of resistance to unjust control. They developed the belief that at the end of time the Imam Mahdi, as the "rightly guided" Imam, will return and introduce a golden era of justice. Until then all authority lies with the "hidden Imam," during which time the legal scholars serve as his earthly representatives.

Only in the Shi'ite community in Iran did a position of spiritual power develop a claim also to political leadership and control. During the Iranian revolution under the leadership of Ayatollah Khomeini, Shi'ite spiritual power for the first time prevailed as the leading political power in Iran. According to the new constitution, the Islamic republic of Iran is based on a list of general Islamic and Shi'ite principles. Among these is the affirmation of the sole sovereignty and legislation of God, the afterlife, and the guarantee of the office and the claim to leadership of the Imam. The legal scholars of the "Assembly of Guardians" check all laws produced by parliament to determine whether they agree with the principles of Islam. During the absence of the hidden Imam, a just legal scholar, who is recognized by the people as such, exercises leaderhip on his behalf.

## RELIGION AND STATE IN MODERN SUNNI ISLAM

The revolution in Iran also encouraged those in the Sunni Muslim world who exercise political power and wish to carry through a revolutionary "Islamic order." In the postcolonial era, the idea of building a just social order on the basis of "Islamic socialism" has held great fascination for a number of leaders (for example, Khadafy in Libya and the leaders of Algeria and Syria). Many conservative rulers in a number of Islamic countries were therefore strengthened in their rule by that revolution and increasingly prevailed against "secular" tendencies within their realms. Penal provisions of traditional Islamic law were reintroduced into several states and applied with great rigor. Militant anti-Western groups and parties, such as the Muslim Brotherhood and the *Jama'at-i Islami* founded by Mawdudi in Pakistan, played an important role. Similar provisions were demanded by the Islamic World League founded in 1962 on Saudi Arabian initiative.

The radical powers mobilized by the Iranian revolution form a revolutionary wing that is generally designated as "Fundamentalism" or "re-Islamization," though both terms are disputed. They strengthen the opposition to those who strive for reform, who wish to adapt Islamic ideas and laws to social change, and who are open to Western ideas insofar as they can be reconciled with Islamic ideals. According to the "Fundamentalist" and "re-Islamizing" revolutionaries, all the problems that the Muslim world is facing today stem from the fact that Muslims have diverged from Islamic principles. They think that by a return to original Islam and by literal adherence to the Qur'an and the sunna, all the problems will be resolved. Currently the reform-oriented leaders face a difficult time. They reject this defensive revolutionary ideology as a distortion of Islam and declare the explanation given to the Muslim identity crisis erroneous. Some of the tensions within Islam reflect the quest for a Muslim identity that will provide a distinctive Muslim way to social justice and economic development that is not the same as Western capitalism. It is a search for an alternative to all kinds of materialism, an alternative that is rooted in the Muslim religion itself and that would reshape economic and social life along lines consistent with Islam.

Chinese Muslims at prayer

# 14

## Groups in Islam

Islam sees itself as a unified and all-encompassing community. In the presence of this unified community (*umma*), Muhammad saw proof that Islam was the true faith. As a consequence, he viewed the division of Christianity in the sixth century as a sign of weakness. In the Qur'an the idea is foreign that a religious community could split into different groups (Sura 9.71). The Qur'an therefore calls people to uphold the unity, "Be not like those who are divided amongst themselves and fall into disputations after receiving clear Signs" (Sura 3.105).

### GROUP FORMATION IN EARLY ISLAM

The first formation of groups had social causes. There were, first of all, tensions between the Muslims who had emigrated from Mecca and the natives of Medina. This caused Muhammad to create laws to fortify unity among the Muslims.

After Muhammad's death, further tensions developed in the argument about his successor, and this led to the formation of smaller groups around different leading personalities. Further divisiveness occurred in 661 when Mu'awiya prevailed in his claim to the Islamic Empire and founded his dynasty following the murder of Ali. The murder of Husayn, one of Ali's sons, in 680 led to the final separation of "Ali's party," the Shi'ites, from the rest of Islamic leadership. The undercurrent of separatism on the part of the Shi'ites deepened as they became increasingly alienated from the Sunnis, and at the same time intra-Sunni tensions increased.

These divisions were a shock for many Muslims. Several attempts at reconciliation failed. For example, the Kharijites refused a court of arbitration in 657 because they believed that only the Qur'an possessed the power to decide an argument. They founded their own community, the *Ibadhites*, who today constitute the majority of Muslims in Oman.

New tensions arose in the eighth century with the development of Islamic law. These were eased somewhat as the Sunnis recognized four legal schools as legitimate. At the same time the public discussion of the question of divine predestination and human free will led to the formation of opposing groups. The Mutazilites emphasized the free will of humans. At first they gained a great following, but could not carry through their rationalistic tendencies. Even today, however, ideas like those held by the Mutazilites are found among Sunnis as well as among the Shi'ites. For the Asharites, in contradistinction to the Mutazilites, the responsibility of humans was limited by the will of God, who determines human behavior.

Theological disputes from the eighth to the tenth centuries led to the formation of new groups. These disputes involved the following issues:

- What attributes does God possess?
- Was the Qur'an in heaven created by God, or was it uncreated, being an eternal expression of divine wisdom?
- What level of importance do Muhammad's sayings and the tradition have for making valid legal decisions?
- How far is it legitimate to summarize and express Islam in a philosophical manner?

During this period numerous mystical orders, which began as ascetic groups, also arose. At first they were seen as sects within Islam. But because they accepted ideas foreign to Islam, such as beliefs that humans can participate in divinity, in many places their leaders were persecuted and in some cases condemned to death. In the eleventh century the theologian Al-Ghazzali made a greatly influential effort to achieve the peaceful coexistence of mysticism and orthodox Islam.

Another factor was the divisiveness of nationalism. Even though the nations shared a common faith, suspicions would arise among Arabs, Iranians, Turks, Mongols, or Kurds about the intentions or actions of other Islamic nations or groups.

## ON THE WAY TO SELF-DISCOVERY

Colonialization of Islamic countries by European powers in the nineteenth and twentieth centuries introduced profound difficulties for the Islamic populations. The new rulers were not Muslims. Furthermore, they introduced new values, such as secular school systems and nonreligious laws. During the colonial period, therefore, numerous nationalist groups arose in the name of liberating Islam from foreign powers.

Many such movements initially had national goals in mind but later developed goals of a more universal kind. They saw and still see their primary duty as the defense of the ancient values of Islam against growing worldliness. They resist the adoption of European value systems, whether they are due to influences from the colonial past or due to current involvements with political and social systems. Such movements often demand that the state system be organized according to Islamic law, call for state support of the *dawah* (Islamic mission), and sometimes even advocate an Islamic economic system.

Some of these groups are skeptical of every form of modernization; others are more or less open-minded. In Europe the imprecise term "Fundamentalists" is often used to designate the radical-conservative groups.

The well-known reformers of the nineteenth century, Jamal ad-Din al-Afghani (1838–1897) and Muhammad Abduh (1849–1905), worked for the renewal of Islam out of its own inner strength. Al-Afghani tried to arouse the Islamic world from its passivity and orient it to the modern technological age in order to again make it competitive with Europe. He called on all Muslims worldwide to join together in a universal Muslim fraternity. Thus he became the father of "pan-Islamism." Al-Afghani and his student Abduh emphasized both the transcendent and the rational aspects of Islam. Reason was to be used in the service of shaping modern Islam, which they perceived as a reasonable and science-friendly faith.

Abduh, who for a time served as a mufti (religious official) and supreme judge in Egypt, furthered these ideas. By means of an independent interpretation of the Qur'an (*ijtihad*) that was oriented to the general good, he strove to modernize Islamic thought, to reform the sharia (traditional law), and to overcome the differences among the four Sunni schools of law. He recommended the use of certain European values within the Islamic community. In his reform efforts, however, he limited himself to his own country.

In 1929 the Muslim Brotherhood was established in Egypt. It has a variety of subgroups in various Islamic countries. They expand on the trends begun by Al-Afghani and Abduh, but do so in a very conservative manner, combining political and religious goals. The Muslim Brotherhood resists what it perceives to be the secular states of Egypt, Syria, and Iraq. Its members also cooperate with Saudi Arabia for tactical reasons. This is a temporary measure, however, since they accuse some leaders as being too ready to compromise. Elsewhere they cooperate with state leaders in an effort to protect Islamic culture from foreign influence.

The party *Jama'at-i Islami* in Pakistan pursues similar goals. It was founded by the Pakistani intellectual leader and politician Abu ala Mawdudi (1903–1979). He crafted his views out of the thought of Al-Afghani, Abduh, and their students. He systematized the Islamic faith into an all-encompassing program that would give due respect to the Qur'an as well as to contemporary demands. Recently groups have arisen in different parts of the Islamic world that orient themselves to Mawdudi's reform ideas.

These efforts in Islamic self-discovery, with an orientation to return to its roots, must be seen against the backdrop of Islam's ongoing argument with the modern world. At the same time as these reform efforts have sprung up, a broad movement of secularization has arisen throughout the Islamic world. This has occurred primarily among the urban and industrial populations and exists with varying degrees of intensity in individual countries. When taken as a whole, Islam has not exclusively rejected the modern world. This fact is reflected in the variety of ways in which there is a positive acceptance of the ideas of Al-Afghani and Abduh.

## AWAITING THE COMING SAVIOR

Some groups place their hope in the coming savior or renewer, the Mahdi. This tradition is disputed in Islam, and among Sunnis it plays only a limited role. Some Mahdi movements are more like spontaneous mass movements with more of a nationalistic than theological origin. In Morocco at the end of the eighteenth century a group arose that honored the Mawla Idris as Muhdi, whose name it bears. Amid political upheaval in Sudan, in 1881 Muhammad Ahmad Ibn as-Sayyid Abd Allah claimed to be the Mahdi and ruled the land for a time. He succeeded in wiping out a British garrison at Khartoum. Later he was attacked and killed by an Anglo-Egyptian army. Today his influence is still noticeable in Sudan.

In connection with the Mahdi expectation, other socially critical groups have arisen, such as Babism in Iran in the nineteenth century. This in turn gave rise to the Baha'i faith beginning in 1863. While Babism is still seen by most Muslims as Islamic, the Baha'is do not regard themselves as such. In fact, the intention of the Baha'i faith is to be understood as a new, universal religion, with the goal of founding a theocratic world government.

The Ahmadiyya movement that arose at the end of the nineteenth century in modern Pakistan is also a group inspired by Mahdiism that claims to be the true Islam. But it is not accepted as part of the Islamic community because it awards its founder Mirza Ghulam Ahmad (d. 1903) with a new prophetic revelation.

That action brings it into conflict with the Islamic teaching that Muhammad was the last prophet.

All these Islamic groups except the Ahmadiyya have access to the international committees and the holy sites of Islam and thus have the recognition of the Islamic world.

## GROUPS IN WESTERN EUROPE

In recent decades large populations from Islamic countries have immigrated to industrial regions of western Europe. They brought their own national peculiarities and the religious groupings from their home countries with them and continue to maintain them in the new environment. Although they still form a social underclass, they are in the process of developing a kind of cohesiveness. The mosque communities and Islamic centers play their part and may be involved in political issues. Nevertheless, most of the Muslim population are more likely to reject any efforts to combine religion and politics.

The diplomatic and economic effects of Islam in general on Europe are to be distinguished from the effect of the immigration of Muslim workers. Islamic states and Islamic organizations, such as the Muslim World League organized by Saudi Arabia, have the opportunity for representation through their consuls, through capital investments, and also through representative mosques and cultural centers.

The influence of fundamentalist groups has undoubtedly also increased in Europe. Influences from Iran as well as the activities of the Muslim Brotherhood and similar groups are welcomed by some of the immigrant Muslims as well as by some Muslims whose families have been in Europe for several generations. Thus a small radical-conservative Islamic group is forming among European Muslims. All of these factors contribute to the absence of any unified image of Islam in Europe. In fact, the whole spectrum of groups and movements in world Islam is represented there.

## GROUPS IN NORTH AMERICA

As mentioned in chapter 8, the two main sources of the growing Muslim presence in North America are (1) African Americans who convert to Islam through the outreach of a number of groups, and (2) immigrant peoples from the Middle East, Asia, Africa, and eastern Europe. For further information, review Part 2 of this book, particularly chapter 8.

# 15

## Islam and the Modern Age

### REACTIONS TO THE ENCOUNTER WITH THE MODERN AGE

The encounter of Islam with modern Western society happened under unfortunate circumstances. It took place when most Islamic countries had come under the control of European colonial powers, or had at least become dependent on these powers. This made the secularizing influence of the modern era appear all the more threatening, culturally alienating, and morally corrosive. These threats are still visible in several areas:

- The ideal of the secular national state contradicted the Islamic understanding of the state and gave new prominence to the old question of the relationship between religion and state as well as between religion and law.
- The individualistic and emancipatory modern ethic was experienced as a danger to traditional morals. This aroused the longing among many Muslims to maintain or enforce such morals once more with state sanctions.

- The economic order of capitalism and liberalism necessarily led to conflict with the Qur'an's prohibition against interest. That brought about the recent efforts to create a specifically Islamic economic system.
- Scientific-technological thinking revived fundamental questions: What is the relationship between divine revelation and human reason, between God's sovereignty and the laws of nature? Such questions in the classical period of Islam led to the conviction that all is established by God and natural laws are to be understood as "God's habits" (that is, rules formulated by the Creator).

These concerns were compounded by the political and ideological demands of socialism and communism.

This double disagreement in the postcolonial period led to Islam's being interpreted as an independent "third way," as an alternative to Western capitalism and Eastern communism. Solutions taken from the West proved to be worthless in solving the problems of Asia and Africa. Islam's resistance can also be seen as a part of the conflict of the "Third World" with the West.

The encounter with the largely secular modern era aroused various reactions in Islam as it did in Hinduism and Buddhism. That these reactions are especially severe in our day is connected with Islam's political and theological character. That double emphasis makes it difficult for Muslims to maintain peaceful coexistence between modern civilization and traditional faith.

Liberal Muslims struggle to reconcile scientific progress and tradition, to integrate new elements into Islam, and to give it a contemporary form. In this struggle, they can refer to the great cultural achievements of their faith in earlier centuries.

Others, in contrast, insist on protecting Islam from foreign influence, which they see as threatening Islam's foundations. The term often used in the West to designate this protective group, Fundamentalist, is perceived as inappropriate by many Muslims.

In any case, all along the spectrum from liberal to conservative, Islam does not remain the same but undergoes transformations. These are only slowly affecting the majority of traditional-minded Muslims, however.

Agreement was reached early on among Muslims that the alienating influence of modernism would not be accepted fatalistically. Since the nineteenth century, both liberal and conservative tendencies appealed equally to the free responsibility of Muslims. They rely on Sura 13.11, "Verily never will Allah change the condition of a people until they change it themselves (with their own souls)." The self-critical search for the "causes of the downfall of the Muslims" is usually answered in the sense of Hassan al-Banna (1906–1949): The "backwardness" of Muslims can be explained by the fact that they have distanced themselves from their faith; the foundation of all reformation must be a return to Islam. Opinions differ as to precisely what that means.

## TRANSFORMATIONS IN MORE RECENT ISLAM

Among the reform movements that referred to the ideal of early Islam, Wahhabism is particularly well known. It is the current state ideology in Saudi Arabia, and its influence is spreading to many Islamic groups. Muhammad ibn Abd al-Wahhab (1703–1787) was the founder, but its spiritual strength derives from Ibn Taymiyah, a theologian and legal scholar of the fourteenth century. Muhammad Wahhab proclaimed an uncompromising position with respect to anything new. His goal was the purification of Islam from all extraneous influences. Any glorification of persons, even the prophet, was rejected. The Qur'an was to be the sole foundation of state law. He turned against all "innovation" (*bida*), by which he meant primarily the glorification of saints' graves and other expressions of folk piety that endangered monotheism. He dismissed blind "imitation" (*taqlid*) of tradition, and promoted *ijtihad*, the "effort of human reason," to find new norms on the basis of an independent interpretation of the Qur'an and tradition. Wahhabism, however, as practiced in its contemporary traditional, conservative shape, does in fact involve a blend of "imitation" and individual "effort."

Islam's encounter with modern Europe began with Napoleon's Egyptian campaign (1798). Among the reformers who reacted to this, Al-Afghani and Abduh are of particular importance. They served as leading figures of modern Islam (see above, pp. 134–35).

Following independence in the Arab countries after World War II, the ideologies of Arab nationalism and socialism (such as that promulgated by Gamal Abdel Nasser, 1918–1970) first dominated. Christians were prominently involved in their development. One example is Michel Aflaq (b. 1912), who was one of the fathers of the socialist Baath Party, which asserted control over the Syrian-Iraqi region. In modern Libya, Arab nationalism and socialism claim to offer a distinct Islamic way.

On the Indian subcontinent, reform movements took other characteristics. Ahmad Khan (1817–1898), known primarily as the founder of the Aligarh University, Amir Ali (1849–1928), and Muhammad Iqbal (1873–1938) favored Western education and science, but at the same time championed an Islamic state as it arose in the form of Pakistan in 1949.

## BETWEEN MODERNIZATION AND ISLAMIZATION

The various reform ideas have been realized only in part. Efforts toward re-Islamization have come to the fore. While some things were taken up, others were rejected as un-Islamic. These efforts began in the 1930s with the (partially subversive) activities of the Muslim Brotherhood and, especially in Pakistan, of the Jama'at-i Islami. These efforts reached a high point with the collapse of the Shah's regime in the Iranian revolution, which was partly a protest against the Shah's move toward westernization, carried out as it was by violent repression. A widespread symbol of these efforts has been the veiling of women's faces. Historically, however, this practice was more cultural than religious in its motivation (orthodox Islam does not require it). Willingness to take on an offensive conflict with the non-Islamic world and to propagate Islam (*dawah*) as the most perfect faith grew under the influence of re-Islamization.

In recent years the internal problems of Islamic countries have come more clearly to the fore. These problems include the shape of an Islamic economy, education, and culture, as well as the problems of the scattered Islamic population in Africa and Western countries. Islamic ideas, like that of unity (*tawhid*), play an important role. This idea does not simply give expression to a theoretical monotheism, but also articulates Islam's concrete claim to give comprehensive guidelines for all aspects of life in the name of God. Economy, culture, and the like should not be ends in themselves, but should be subject to God's will. According to Sura 2.30 ("I will create a vice-regent on earth"), humans are described as God's vice-regents (caliphs).

Today this idea is also emphasized in order to make clear one's ecological obligation. In modern Islam the responsibility of humans to God is interpreted on the basis of Sura 33.72: following completion of creation, God first offered responsibility "to the Heavens and the Earth and the Mountains; but they refused to undertake it, being afraid thereof: But man undertook it—he was indeed unjust and foolish."

## ISLAMIC ECONOMIC METHODS

The fundamentals of an Islamic economic theory are freedom of decision making and the responsibility of the individual associated with this, together with unity and balance. Social justice, equality, and simplicity of life-style are also often named. God serves as the sole proprietor of all earthly goods; humans are only trustees. These fundamentals are hardly distinguishable from the rules of Christian economic ethics once developed by the church fathers. The opinions of the Muslim economic theorists differ when it comes to practical application. Some come close to an economic system that builds on the ethical demands of the Qur'an and applies these directly to the present. Traditional Muslims, on the other hand, would like to retain certain prescriptions from tradition and support the reintroduction of social contributions into the tax system. The Qur'an's prohibition against accepting *riba*, translated as "interest" or "profiteering," has led to attempts to create an Islamic banking system in which interest income is replaced by profit sharing or something similar. Muslims agree that the economy must remain subject to the demands of Islamic ethics.

The Islamic understanding of unity (*tawhid*) affirms a unity between faith and science, revelation and reason, religion and lifestyle. As times change, this can lead to new tensions. Today, in some Islamic circles, *tawhid* is interpreted in such a rigorous and narrow way that it becomes difficult to respond to the demands of the modern world—scientific freedom, a pluralistic worldview, human rights, the liberation of women. Muslims in many places lament such a defensive position, in which they see a political misuse of religion.

# PART FOUR

# Islam and Christianity

# 16

# Christian-Islamic Encounters in History

Christians and Muslims have lived in one another's immediate vicinity since the start of Islam in the seventh century. While political history between them has been shaped by opposition, on the cultural and religious level there have been recurring fruitful exchanges despite profound differences.

## THE EARLY PERIOD IN THE NEAR EAST

From the Qur'an we can tell that the first encounters between Christians and Muslims were characterized by mutual tolerance despite religious differences of opinion. This is made clear, for example, in the encounter between Muhammad and a delegation of Christians from south Arabia. Muhammad wanted to unite into one community all who believe in the one true God. When the Christians could not agree to this and rejected arranging for a "judgment of God," this question was "postponed" (see Sura 5.48ff.).

The Christians in Syria and Egypt, who distinguished them-selves from the Greek Orthodox imperial church in Constantinople because of dogmatic conflicts over the person of Jesus (monophy-sitism), were persecuted by the church and in fact received the Muslim conquerors as liberators. They were seen as "protected ones" under Islamic rule, with the right to freedom of religion, but with limits to their civil rights. In the following period many of them converted to Islam, although the Muslims hardly encouraged conversion, because then the poll tax (*jizyah*) that all adult non-Muslims had to pay was eliminated.

Christians at the time were hardly aware of the importance of Islam as a new world religion. The Greek Orthodox church father John of Damascus (d. ca. 750), whose father was a civil servant at the caliphal court of Damascus, understood Islam as a Christian sect and compared it with Arianism, which one-sidedly emphasized the humanity of Jesus. Islam was viewed, like other sects, as a sign that the Antichrist would come soon.

At the court of the Abbasid caliph (after 753) in Baghdad, Christian scholars gained great respect. The best-known conver-sation about religion of this epoch took place in the year 782 between the caliph Al-Mahdi and the Nestorian patriarch Timotheus I. The patriarch respected the ethical progress that Muhammad's proc-lamation had effected among Arabs, but declined to recognize Mu-hammad as the Prophet, whose coming Muslims say is foreshad-owed in the Bible.

Despite lively dialogues on philosophical and theological questions, occasional political measures were taken against Chris-tians. These measures were intended to make the societal position of Christians more difficult. Yet in the first three Islamic centuries, larger disputes seldom occured; a rebellion of the Copts in Egypt did occur in 829–830. This relative harmony changed with the de-cline in power of the caliphal court in Baghdad in the tenth century.

## SPAIN AND SICILY

In the year 711 Muslims crossed the Straits of Gibraltar. The empire of the West Goths was destroyed. In the following centuries a series of Islamic empires were established on the Iberian Peninsula; their cities became centers of lively scientific and philosophical scholarship. Muslim as well as Jewish scholars studied ancient Greek and Indian natural science, literature, and philosophy, and developed these areas further.

In the Islamic West, the Christians in Spain and North Africa were primarily descendants of the old Iberian population. They adopted the Arabic language and culture without becoming Muslim. Many ancient (originally Greek) texts, available only in Arabic by this time, were translated into Latin and became the foundation for the medieval science of western Europe.

Despite internal political confusions and the progressive Christian reconquest of Spain, another cultural high point, especially in philosophy and medicine, came with the philosopher Ibn Rushd (Averroes, 1126–1198), the mystic Muhyi ad-din ibn al-Arabi (1165–1240), and the Jewish philosopher Moses Maimonides (1135–1204). This period of fruitful exchange came to an end when Granada was conquered in 1492 with the subsequent expulsion of all non-Christians from Spain.

Sicily too was under Islamic rule for a time (831–1072). Although this was a relatively short period, the cultural influences long remained and reached as far as southern Italy. The Staufer emperor Frederick II (1194–1250) was a political opponent of the Saracens, but he cultivated Moorish culture at his court in Palermo.

## THE PERIOD OF THE CRUSADES

While Emperor Charlemagne (d. 814) had kept up diplomatic contacts with the caliph Harun ar-Rashid in Baghdad, in 1095 Pope Urban II introduced a new phase in history with his call for the First Crusade to the Holy Land. It led to the encounter of Muslims with the new Christians of western Europe, usually called the Franks.

The Franks viewed Muslims as soldiers of the Antichrist and also saw the Near Eastern Christians as heretics. The blood bath that followed the Crusaders' capture of Jerusalem in 1099 claimed countless victims among Muslim, Jewish, and Christian populations.

The idea of the Crusades, the liberation of the Holy Land and of Christ's grave from the hands of the infidel, led to the belief among Muslims that the cross was a symbol of Western-Christian aggression and barbarism. The Crusader states in the Middle East were not least the result of political and economic expansion. Near Eastern Christians also suffered at the hands of the Crusaders, yet Muslims increasingly doubted the Christians' loyalty to them. Thus the situation of Near Eastern Christians continued to deteriorate.

As a result of the Crusades a flood of propaganda was created in western Europe that defamed Islam and condemned the person of Muhammad as immoral. These vilifying stereotypes still have an effect today.

## INTELLECTUAL DEBATE IN THE MIDDLE AGES

There were also voices within the Christian world that opposed a conflict with Islam on the battlefield. They called rather for an intellectual debate.

The abbot of the reform cloister at Cluny in southern France, Petrus Venerabilis, allowed a translation of the Qur'an to be made in 1143. With its help he attempted to fight "against the abominable heresy of the sect of the Saracens" with love, not with weapons.

Francis of Assisi (1182–1226) did not want to fight Muslims but to convert them. For this purpose he traveled several times to the Near East. His integrity and spiritual power earned him respect among Muslims because he defended his own faith without at the same time disdaining theirs.

Raymond Lull (1235–1315) repeatedly traveled as a missionary to North Africa. His excellent knowledge of Arabic and of the Qur'an brought him respect. He succeeded in getting the Council of Vienne in 1312 to approve the establishment of teaching positions in Semitic languages at five European universities (Bologna, Salamanca, Avignon, Paris, and Oxford).

Christian theology in the late Middle Ages received a substantial contribution from Islam. The work of Aristotle, which had been lost in the West, again became known through the translation work of scholars, many of them Muslims, who knew Arabic. In the dispute with Aristotle and with Islamic-Arabic philosophy influenced by him, the renowned theologian Thomas Aquinas (1225–1274) wrote his text against the heathens, *Summa contra Gentiles*. Roger Bacon (ca. 1214–1294) rejected the attempt to dispose of Islam by war. The souls of the subjects could not thus be won for the Christian faith. His student, John of Segovia, even said that Christianity must not lead any wars because doing so would contradict its spirit.

The turn to mysticism and asceticism led both sides to greater mutual understanding in the thirteenth century. For Joachim of Floris (d. 1202), Islam was one of the three last great scourges to afflict the church. The last great enemy for him, however, was Rome, within Christianity itself.

Toward the end of the Middle Ages, Cardinal Nicholas of Cusa (1401–1464) expressly espoused the cause of better relations with Islam. He supported "conferences" between Christians and Muslims. At these the goal was to study what was essential and good in both faiths. He himself studied the Qur'an for this purpose and above all found its ethical challenges exemplary.

## THE REFORMATION PERIOD

The new thinking of the Reformation led to no fundamental change in the understanding of Islam. Martin Luther (1483–1546) and his contemporaries experienced the violent threat of the Turks on the Balkans, but rejected a religious basis for the battle against the Turks. He understood them as an example of a "rod of correction" with which God punishes Christians for their "entanglement in sinfulness." In this situation "nothing is achieved with our strength"; only repentance could bring a change. On the basis of reports of returned prisoners of war, Luther praised the high ethical standard of Muslims and their sense of justice. But theologically he rejected Islam, like the Papacy and the Jewish faith, as a form of works righteousness that put Christ's work of redemption in question. Still he supported the efforts of the Swiss scholar Bibliander to produce a new edition of the Qur'an translated by Petrus Venerabilis and to reprint it, despite severe opposition on the part of the Protestant councilmen of Zurich and Basel. He wrote a lengthy introduction for it in 1543. It was intended to serve scholarly debate.

## THE ENLIGHTENMENT

Not until the Enlightenment did the approach to Islam change substantially. The teachers of Arabic and Semitic languages attempted to be free themselves of the tutelage of the theological faculties. The Italian scholar Ludovico Maracci published a new Qur'an translation in 1698 in which he strove for philological accuracy. New impressions of the Near East were conveyed by pilgrims, travelers, and merchants. Likewise Muslims from the Balkans came to the West. Some even served in the Prussian army. The Enlightenment led to skepticism with regard to the truth claims of historical religions while also demanding religious tolerance. People believed that significant ethical values could be found through reason in a higher "natural religion," which is manifested only piecemeal in historical religions. This is made clear, for example, in the famous "parable of the rings" in the play by G. E. Lessing, *Nathan the Wise* (1779). Many thought that the proof as to whether Judaism, Christianity, or Islam is the true faith would be shown by the ethical behavior of their adherents.

## THE CAMPAIGN OF NAPOLEON AND
## ITS RESULTS

In 1798 Napoleon undertook a military expedition to Egypt, which had many consequences. His retinue included scholars who had studied the ancient culture of Egypt as well as its Islamic civilization and who had made efforts to make contacts with Egyptian scholars. Although the military action failed, after Muhammad Ali took over power in Cairo (1804–1848), largely independent of the Ottoman Empire, the cultural and military-technological connections with the French were resumed. The French delivered printing presses with Arabic letters so that for the first time the classical texts of Islam—with the exception of the Qur'an—could be printed and distributed in great numbers. Doctors, biologists, and agronomists, primarily from Austria-Hungary, were attracted to this new intellectual stimulation. Al-Jabarti, an Egyptian eyewitness of Napoleon's invasion, described the often curious impressions that European civilization made on the Egyptians. Students sent to Europe also reported on their experiences and aroused serious thought about the social, intellectual, and religious situation in their home country.

## THE PERIOD OF WESTERN COLONIAL RULE

Napoleon's Egyptian campaign was the prelude not only to increased cultural encounters but also to the colonial invasion of the Islamic world by Europeans (*ifranj*, Franconians), who for Muslims were at the same time representatives of Christianity. The French conquered Algeria in 1830; later Tunisia and Morocco came under French dominion.

The British were interested in Egypt primarily as a land bridge between the Red Sea and the Mediterranean in order to reach their colonies in East and South Africa. The Dutch brought the most populous Islamic region under their rule when they took over control of the islands of Southeast Asia (especially Indonesia). By often sending the leaders of rebellious Islamic groups into exile, they were instrumental in spreading Islam into other countries as well. For example, Javanese workers emigrated to South Africa (Cape Town) and Suriname.

The British subdued the last supporters of the Islamic mogul rule in 1857 and thus solidified their control of India. Following completion of the Suez Canal (1869) and the state bankruptcy of Egypt (1879), the British and French secured the majority of stocks and thus supremacy over this important waterway. Finally, following victory over the Ottoman Empire in World War I, they divided the newly "free" Arab provinces (Syria, Lebanon, Iraq, Palestine, Transjordan) among themselves as "spheres of influence" and thus were decisively involved in the development of a Near East crisis that continues to the present.

## CONSEQUENCES FOR CHRISTIANS OF THE NEAR EAST

The period of Western rule over most of the Islamic countries, and especially the disdain for human dignity connected with it, left deep wounds in Muslim perceptions of European Christians. At the same time Muslim relations with Near Eastern Christians were also at times burdened or even poisoned by a similar attitude toward Muslims.

Christians themselves also suffered under Europeans' general superciliousness toward "Near Easterners," since most of the Christians in the Near East belonged to churches that Europeans considered heretical. Many a mission society, after having had little success among Muslims, turned to Near Eastern Christians in order to make them "better" Christians. But there were also positive influences. For instance, the Copts in Egypt modernized their education system primarily through their own efforts as promoted by the "reform patriarch" of their church, Cyril IV (1854–1861). Many civil servants and employees in the economic and finance ministries were Copts, and their number among academics was relatively high. Despite their openness to Western knowledge, most of them remained faithful to their own church tradition and maintained close relations with Muslim intellectuals and literary scholars with whom they shared their love of a common homeland.

Like the Egyptians, the Syrians also strove for a common renaissance of Arab culture and worked together in publications and political parties as well. Since the colonial governments opposed provisions in Islamic law that discriminated against non-Muslims, Near Eastern Christians did support those governments. This led to a certain mistrust among Muslims regarding the Christians' loyalty. Thus during uprisings of anticolonial unrest, there were repeated excesses against local Christians, of whom many decided to emigrate.

## THE WESTERN IMAGE OF THE
## NEAR EAST

Not only was political oppression degrading for Muslims, but they were increasingly viewed and treated by Europeans according to two conflicting viewpoints. On the one hand, educated Europeans cultivated an idealized image of a once-progressive and high civilization on the basis of their increased research into classical Islamic philosophy and scientific literature. On the other hand, travelers, pilgrims, and even scholars returning from the Near East reported the backwardness, superstition, and "primitiveness" of Near Eastern people and their living conditions. These reports were considered tantamount to descriptions of Islam. Thus the conviction grew that Islam had used up the power it once had and must now yield to the advance of Western civilization and religion.

Stereotypes about the Near East and its exoticism arose: chivalrous and spoiled, romantic and repulsive, as depicted for instance in *The Arabian Nights* by Karl May. Attempts were seldom made to understand the people of the Near East in their own environment. Even their impressive literary inheritance was interpreted according to the values of Western criticism.

For example, the French philosopher and linguist Ernest Renan (1823–1892) reshaped the criticism of the Muslim philosopher Ibn Rushd (Averroes) into a general criticism of religion, which he had originally applied to the method of traditional Islamic theology. Renan was not interested in faithfully rendering Ibn Rushd's opinion, but was interested in the fact that Thomas Aquinas had already written against Ibn Rushd and also had recognized the "antago-nism" between philosophy and theology.

Yet there were also positive attempts to be fair to the cultural inheritance of the Near East, for example through the members of the German Near Eastern Society. One of its founders, the poet Friedrich Ruckert (1788–1866), translated portions of the Qur'an into poetic German.


## THE ATTITUDE OF WESTERN
## CHRISTIANS

From the beginning of the nineteenth century until recently, West-ern churches and mission societies had been of the opinion that Islam had no future. Many theologians held an opinion similar to that of the missionary Karl Gottlieb Pfander (1803–1865), who worked in Persia and India. He believed the time was ripe to prove the superiority of Christianity over Islam through correctly chosen arguments. He attempted this in his book *The Scales of Truth*, which was translated into various Near Eastern languages. At the first World Mission Conference in 1910 in Edinburgh, the belief in the impending disintegration of Islam also dominated. Such thinking was related to the expected collapse of the Ottoman Empire. This hope for disintegration was ill-founded. After the victory over the Ottomans and the dissolution of their empire, there was an in-creasing revival of Islamic thought. At the second World Missionary Conference in Jerusalem in 1928, the participants saw their error; some of them now even viewed Islam as a possible partner in the expected debates with materialistic thought influenced by Marxism.

Aside from Pfander, other missionaries brought a greater re-spect for Islam. The English missionary Henry Martyn attempted dialogue with educated Muslims in India; the North American missionary Samuel Zwemer studied the Islam of Arabia and taught at the University of Cairo. On Zwemer's initiative the journal *Mus-lim World* was founded in 1911 following the Edinburgh conference; it is still among the most significant scholarly journals on Islam. The French Protestant missionary Jean Faure (1907–1967) attempted to live together with Muslims in Morocco, similar to the Catholic white fathers in East and North Africa. Muslims also recognized that missionaries frequently numbered among the critics and opponents of colonial politics.


## MUHAMMAD IN CHRISTIAN PERSPECTIVE

For philosophers as well as theologians of the nineteenth century, Muhammad and the Qur'an were the actual causes for the perceived failure of Islam. The dogmatically and morally distorted image of Muhammad from the Middle Ages and the Reformation was accepted as the truth for the most part, occasionally supported by various findings of more recent historical study. Only Thomas Carlyle (1795–1881), influenced by Romanticism, tried to form a positive understanding of Muhammad and his importance for the reordering of his time. Yet his "hero," as Carlyle depicted Muhammad, was more closely related to Carlyle's own understanding of hero than to the historical person.

Other researchers also placed the accents to suit their own interests. Hubert Grimme in his Muhammad biography (vol. 1, 1892) praised above all Muhammad's social views. The first appreciation for the Prophet's religious ideas came in work on the biography of Muhammad of the Scandinavian researchers Frants Buhl (1903) and Tor Andrae (1930).

Despite all of the historical research, the image of Muhammad of most Europeans remains ahistorical. Unfounded Western criticism generates greater Muslim support for their Prophet. Since about 1930 Islamic scholars and literary critics have been trying to describe and present the person of Muhammad and his inspiration and effect on history as an important model, especially for youth.


## BEGINNINGS OF A NEW MOVEMENT

Since the end of World War II, Christians and Muslims have been seeing, more clearly than before, that as neighbors they must work more closely together in politics, economy, culture, and religion. For this reason, a new consideration of the character of their relationship is required. Within the Roman Catholic Church the Second Vatican Council referred to the common roots of Judaism, Christianity, and Islam in the traditions that go back to the "father of faith," Abraham. The World Council of Churches (WCC) has organized meetings between Muslims and Christians, most recently in Colombo, Sri Lanka, 1982. The effort is not to mix the two religions, but to discuss common questions and to reach deeper understanding and respect. The General Secretary of the Islamic World Congress permitted an official visit of the General Secretary of the WCC. On major holidays, greetings are exchanged between church and Islamic dignitaries. Numerous regional and local meetings are arranged in order to mutually dismantle prejudices.

# 17

# Jerusalem—The City of Three Faiths

Judaism, Christianity, and Islam are all connected with Jerusalem through Abraham. According to the biblical tradition, Melchizedek, the mysterious ancient King of Salem (Salem = Jerusalem), greeted Abraham with bread and wine and blessed him (Gen. 14:18-20).

According to Jewish tradition, in the land of Moriah was the mountain where Abraham took Isaac in order to give his son back to God in that most difficult test of obedience (Gen. 22:2). This location later became the temple mount of Jerusalem. Muslims remember this in connection with the pilgrimage to Mecca when they celebrate the sacrificial feast, the *Id-al-Adha;* they, too, know that the test of obedience happened on the same temple mount.

According to the New Testament, Abraham is "to those who share the faith . . . the father of all of us" (Rom. 4:16). In the Qur'an, among the Old Testament prophets, and in the New Testament he is called friend of God (Sura 4.125; Isa. 41:8, James 2:23).

## JERUSALEM (JERUSHALIYIM), THE
## CITY OF ISRAEL

David conquered the Jebusite city of Jerusalem and made it the
center of the united Israelite tribal kingdom about one thousand
years before Christ. This occurred several centuries after Israel took
the land of Canaan (Palestine). David brought the ark of the covenant, the sign of the presence of God, to "his city," thereby making
it a religious center (2 Sam. 6:1-15). In a crisis, the holiness of the
hill became clear to him (2 Sam. 24:10-25). Later his son Solomon
built the first temple there.

Israel was convinced that God's "gracious presence" abided
there. Pilgrims at the annual pilgrimage sang "Pray for the peace
of Jerusalem" (Ps. 122:6). Jerusalem and the temple were seen as
one. To take part in the worship community meant to be near to
the mercy of God, to receive forgiveness through the sacrifices,
and to receive God's instructions (Torah) through the priests and
prophets. Jerusalem also played a role in Israel's vision of the future:
One day all peoples will make their way to Mount Zion (one of
the hills where Jerusalem stands), "the mountain of the LORD . . .
that he may teach us his ways . . . neither shall they learn war any
more" (Isa. 2:1-4; Mic. 4:1-4).

The destruction of Jerusalem and the temple was thus a tre-
mendous blow to Israel. The first destruction occurred in 587 B.C.
at the hands of the Babylonians. Not until seventy-two years later
could a new, much humbler temple be dedicated (Ezra 6:15). It
took five hundred years until Herod replaced it with characteristic
splendor in ten years' building time. This was shortly before the
birth of Jesus. At that time the square on the temple mount was
expanded to its present size. With the destruction of the temple
and the conquering of Jerusalem by the Romans under Titus in
A.D. 70 and the destruction of the entire city by Hadrian in A.D.
135 after putting down the insurrection of Bar Kochba, Jews were
prohibited from entering Jerusalem. Hadrian founded an entirely
new city, Colonia Aelia Capitolina. On the temple mount stood a
statue of him as emperor. From this time onward, Jews could only
exist as a minority in the city. But even after they had been dispersed

as far as China, the city remained the object of their longings. Jews wish one another "Next year in Jerusalem!" at the end of the annual Passover festival. Often they were not permitted to bring their petitions and laments before God to a part of the western retaining wall, the Wailing Wall.

For contemporary Israel, Jerusalem is the location of the merciful presence of God, represented by the temple mount in the Islamic old part of the city. As the Israeli troops stood before the Wailing Wall on July 12, 1967, the Israeli defense minister Moshe Dayan declared, "We have returned to that which is holy in our land. We have come in order that we should never again be separated from it."

## JERUSALEM (HIEROSOLYMA), THE CITY OF CHRISTIANS

For Christians, Jerusalem is, above all, connected with the life of Jesus. When old Simeon saw the infant Jesus he praised God in the temple: "My eyes have seen your salvation, which you have prepared in the presence of all peoples" (Luke 2:30-31). The story of the twelve-year-old Jesus at the temple demonstrates that the Christian church can never be separated from Israel's experience of God (Luke 2:41-50).

When Jesus cleansed the temple to be "a house of prayer for all the nations" (Mark 11:17; compare Isa. 56:7), some of the people turned against him. The path began there that led to his being taken prisoner in Gethsemane, to a hearing with the high priest, to conviction by the Roman occupying force, and to execution "outside the city gate" (Heb. 13:12), on the cliffs of Golgotha near an unused grave. This ground became a part of the city a few years after Jesus' death. The original community lived in Jerusalem.

With the acceptance of Christianity by Constantine, on the initiative of the emperor's mother Helena, a "church of the holy sepulchre" was built over the grave and cliff as a place to worship Christ. Eastern Orthodox Christians call it the Church of the Holy Sepulchre. The bond of the Orthodox Church to the place of Jesus' execution and burial is similar to the bond that ties the Jewish tradition to Mount Zion. For through Jesus, the "shoot from the root of Jesse" of the house of David, God's mercy for all people becomes real. In the New Testament, the earthly city prefigures the "heavenly Jerusalem," where peace and justice abide. Nevertheless, the earthly Jerusalem has remained a place of pious veneration.

## JERUSALEM (AL-QUDS), THE CITY OF MUSLIMS

Islamic reports relate that the Christian patriarch Sophronios asked Caliph Umar in 638 to take over the city in order to protect it from attack and looting by Arab armies. Thereupon, Umar hurried from Medina and entered Jerusalem, intentionally without pomp. In a protective contract, he assured Christians of continued use of all churches and places of pilgrimage and the free expression of religion. The story is told that as Umar was viewing the Church of the Holy Sepulchre, the hour of ritual prayer came. The caliph turned down the invitation to pray there but did go into the church with the patriarch. He did not want Muslims to turn the church into a mosque on the excuse that he had prayed there.

For Umar, the Islamic occupation of the city was final. At that time he determined that an unused space on the temple square should become the site of the first mosque. The legend tells that a local Jew helped him in his search for the holy rock buried under rubble. But in the traditions concerning Muhammad's recollection of his visionary nighttime travel to Jerusalem (*isra*) and being carried off to heaven (*miraj*), Umar himself rediscovered the rock and the cave under the rock plate. There the messenger Muhammad is supposed to have met the earlier prophets, including Abraham, Moses, and Jesus, and led them in prayer.

These traditions show that Muslims trace the importance that Jerusalem has for them back to Muhammad. They call the city Al-Quds, "the holy city" (actually *al-Bayt al-Muqaddas*, "the Holy House"). Jerusalem is for them the third most important city of pilgrimage, next to Mecca and Medina. Early Muslims looked toward Jerusalem in prayer. Not until the emigration to Medina in 622 was the original prayer direction changed to Mecca. But, at the end of time, the Kaaba of Mecca is to be married as a "holy bride" to her bridegroom, the "holy rock" of the temple mount.

Muslims lost no time making their claims on the city visible through construction. Fifty-four years after Umar's entry, the caliphs of the Umayyad dynasty completed the Dome of the Rock over the "holy rock." This was the first representative structure of Islam ever built. A few years later the Al-Aqsa mosque was built. The building is arranged so that Muslims perform their prayer in the direction of Mecca with their back to the location of the Jewish temple, indicating their separation from that which marks the holiness of the Jews. At the same time, the buildings exceeded the size and splendor of the earlier Church of the Holy Sepulchre. The Qur'anic inscriptions concerning Jesus inscribed at the Dome of the Rock are intended clearly to demarcate their understanding from that of the declarations made by the Christian community.

Later history brought periods of generous tolerance. The Abbasid caliph Harun al-Rashid, for example, gave Charlemagne the keys to the city of Jerusalem in his coronation year (800) so that he could arrange for good accommodations as well as protection of the pilgrims and the city's churches. Jews also were permitted in this period to move their high council from Tiber back to Jerusalem. At other times, heavy persecution caused considerable damage to mutual relationships. In the year 1009, the Egyptian Fatimid caliph Al-Hakim permitted the demolition of the Church of the Holy Sepulchre (among others), contrary to the word and spirit of the Qur'an. Reconstruction would only be completed during the Crusades.

The century of the Crusaders' rule was full of terror. On conquering the city in 1099, the Crusaders committed an indescribable massacre, a downright decimation of the Jews, Eastern Christians, and Muslims. No Muslim or Jew was permitted to remain in the city—not even later in 1229, when Emperor Frederick II reigned in Jerusalem for fifteen years during the "bloodless crusade." In contrast, Saladin had already reconfirmed the letter of protection of Caliph Umar during his reconquest in 1187.

After Sultan Selim I conquered Jerusalem and Egypt in 1516–17, ushering in the four-hundred-year Turkish rule over Palestine, his son, Suleyman the Magnificent, had the western or Wailing Wall reexposed and allowed Jews access to it.

Through renovations and wall construction, Suleyman shaped the appearance of the old part of the city as it still appears today. At the same time Turkish troops protected pilgrims from attack by Bedouins. Jerusalem, however, declined in importance.

Not until the early nineteenth century did the city get a chance to develop itself anew through the strengthening of Egypt and reforms in Istanbul. These made Jewish immigration from European countries possible. Political influence from Europe also led to the establishment of Western churches, the foundation of a new bishopric of the Anglican church, established jointly by the English parliament and the Protestant King of Prussia in Jerusalem in 1841, and a "Latin" (Roman Catholic) patriarchate in 1847. The Jewish population was able to reinforce its jurisdiction with a head rabbi. Toward the end of World War I, the British wrested control of Jerusalem from the collapsing Ottoman Empire.

## THE COMMON JERUSALEM—A CITY OF PEACE?

With the Balfour Declaration of the British government in 1917, a "national homeland in Palestine" was promised to the Jewish people without infringing the civil and religious rights of the non-Jewish communities already existing in Palestine. Upon the United Nations proclamation of the state of Israel in 1948, the Jews referred back to this promise. After the resulting battles, Jerusalem became a divided city. The eastern part remained inaccessible to Israelis until Israel captured it in the war of 1967. "The reunification of Jerusalem can never be relinquished," say the Israelis. "We cannot tolerate occupation," respond the Arabs—Muslims as well as Christians.

The Jewish faith cannot do without Jerusalem. Its roots are deeply connected with the land and "the city of our God." Throughout the many centuries of diaspora among the nations the curse against oneself continues to resound: "If I forget you, O Jerusalem, let my right hand wither!" (Ps. 137:5). The question debated among Jews is whether or not ownership of the temple mountain in the Islamic eastern part of the city is necessary for the completion of their return to the ancestral land, making it possible for the full messianic salvation of God to dawn.

For Muslims, too, Al-Quds (Jerusalem) with its *al-Haram ash-sharif* (temple mount, "the Noble Sanctuary" and Al-Aqsa mosque) is a holy place, never to be relinquished. According to the Qur'an, Muhammad was carried off into heaven from this site (Sura 17.1). The people believe it is here that the final judgment will take place and the gate of paradise will open.

For the ecumenical community of Christians, Jerusalem is and remains the place where the suffering and resurrection of Jesus Christ took place.

Jerusalem today is a demonstration of the difficulty of the three faiths' realizing peace. At the same time the city remains a place of promise and expectation that it is God who will create peace. For this reason Jews, Christians, and Muslims are obligated to seek reconciliation among themselves.

AN EGYPTIAN MOSQUE

# 18

# Marriages between Christians and Muslims

In marriages between Christians and Muslims, the multifaceted problems of the encounter between two religions and cultures are pronounced. Such problems include the differences in legal systems and perceptions of justice, convictions about family and family discipline, the relationship between religion and society, and also the response to change in religious life brought about by the influences of modern industrial society. The following problem areas in particular arise:

- the legal framework for such a marriage
- differing understandings of male and female roles
- guidelines for educating children and youth, questions of religious affiliation for them, and the place of legal and spiritual counsel
- free practice of faith for both marriage partners who are of different faiths
- conversion of one partner to the faith of the other, generally that of the husband

A matter of critical importance is whether this marriage takes place in a Western-influenced country or in a traditional Islamic country. While each marriage is unique, the fundamental understanding of marriage in Islam influences all aspects. This was described in chapter 6, "Woman and Family."

## TWO CULTURES

In Europe the number of Muslim men who marry Christian women is ten times higher than that of Muslim women who marry Christian men. It is generally the men who have left their homelands and married in a foreign country. Male domination in marriage is often the cultural tradition. This can lead to a husband making demands to which his wife is not accustomed. In Western countries, which also have a tradition of male dominance, the notion of equal partnership is increasingly the norm. Muslim wives may have trouble handling the demands this equal partnership puts on them, and Muslim husbands have to deal with their partners' assumptions about equality.

If the couple lives in an Islamic country, the structures of the dominant society will also influence their relationship. Being prepared to deal with this influence is decisive for the success or failure of the relationship. The partner coming from the West will have to learn to accept the intensive network of societal and familial connections into which this marriage is tied and to adjust to them. For the wife this means subordinating herself to the hierarchy of the older women in the extended family; for the husband, it means recognizing the superior position of the older men and recognizing the involvement of the extended family in decisions within the marriage. This is the case not only in towns but also in cities, although the trend away from extended families and toward nuclear families is increasing. The Christian partner is expected to identify with the Islamic family and to support the honor of the extended family. Then he or she will receive help and protection. If this integration does not happen, there is the danger that the new partner will be isolated.

There can be particular difficulties if the wife wants to have a career. A high value is placed on a wife's role in home and family.

Islam also does not discourage women from having a career. In certain cultural traditions, however, this may be considered threatening to the husband's reputation—if she earns her own income it is as if the husband is incapable of providing a lifestyle appropriate for his wife.

## TWO RELIGIONS

Religious questions are often not at the forefront of a marriage because people have learned to know and value an apparently secular world, free of religion. In the course of marriage, however, questions do come up that may be unexpected. There can be conflicts, for example, about the question of keeping the Muslim food commandments (prohibition of pork and alcohol).

The Muslim father, according to tradition, must whisper the Islamic call to prayer and the confession of faith, the *shahadah*, into the ear of his newborn child when he first holds it in his arms. In his eyes the child is born Muslim. According to Islamic law and practice, children from a Christian-Muslim marriage are to become Muslim, and normally a Muslim man will discuss the raising of children as Muslim with his wife-to-be before marriage. For the Christian mother there is the timeless command to baptize (Matt. 28:19). Even if the mother postpones the question of baptism, it may still be present in her subconscious and may burden her conscience. The obligation to give her child a Christian upbringing may continue to trouble her.

The yearly pattern of holidays repeatedly raises questions: Do I as a wife belong to the faith of my husband? Do I as a husband belong to the faith of my wife? Suddenly the differences between the religions become painfully obvious. It begins very practically: How does one celebrate Christian holidays such as Christmas and Easter in an Islamic environment, and the Muslim holidays *Id-al-Fitr* (the Little Feast) and *Id-al-Adha* (the Feast of Sacrifice) in a Christian environment? How does one practice the behavior required during Ramadan in a Christian environment?

The question may also arise of whether it is time for one partner to convert—even if only with the goal of stabilizing the marriage. The Qur'an does not demand conversion in the marriage of a Christian woman to a Muslim (Sura 5.5) and emphasizes: "Let there be no compulsion in religion" (Sura 2.256). The Muslim husband must permit his Christian wife to participate in the worship of her faith. The situation is similar in the Malikite school. Yet many Muslims hope that conversion will be the logical result of a marriage between a Christian woman and a Muslim man.

Many Protestant churches in Europe offer help for Christian-Muslim couples beginning their path together in the form of a "worship service on the occasion of marriage between a Christian and a non-Christian." In it God's promise for marriage is expressed and God's blessing requested for the couple. Preparatory conversations with the pastor are a prerequisite for such a worship service. In these the non-Christian is to learn the Christian understanding of marriage as a bond entered into before God " 'til death do you part"; at the same time both parties are to commit to a monogamous marriage and permit each other free practice of faith. On the question of children, an arrangement is to be found that is satisfactory to both parties, so that the children will be able to learn about the religious traditions of both parents.

Muslims offer a "marriage in the mosque." It is common that the imam recites the first sura of the Qur'an and confirms the mutual marriage contract. If the Christian partner is called on to say the Islamic confession of faith, the *shahadah*, and complies, then he or she is considered converted to Islam. According to Islamic understanding, this step is irrevocable.


## IN THE GERMAN SETTING

In Germany a marriage is not valid unless it is concluded in a civil ceremony. But even a valid marriage recognized by the state is not enough to permit a foreign partner residency. If the pair wants to live in Germany they must become informed about the requirements of the foreign law and its administrative requirements. The marriage of a German woman to a husband of another nationality is subject to international private law with varying national arrangements. If the foreign husband requests a divorce, in Germany the decision is made according to the law of the country where the married couple primarily lived. This means that the law of another country can be applied in Germany.

## IN NORTH AMERICA

In the United States, although a few uniform laws exist, rules regarding marriage and divorce are state governed. The laws are the same for all people, including Muslims. If a person from another country—say, a Muslim student from Saudi Arabia—marries an American, the marriage is not sufficient to estabish residency or citizenship. The noncitizen would need to meet other requirements for residency or for becoming an American citizen.

Laws about divorce vary, but states usually have a residency requirement, perhaps 180 days. Some uniform rules do exist, for example, those regarding payment of child support. Regulations about other issues, such as grounds for divorce, are likely to differ. Muslims are subject to the same laws as everyone else and would need to check the laws in their state of residence.

## IN ISLAMIC COUNTRIES

In Islamic countries—excepting Turkey and a few others that officially require civil marriages—marriage is fundamentally a private contract. Marriage is seen as a covenant with God. The family of the bride secures the rights of the future wife through arrangement of a contract, for which there are state-recognized models. It goes beyond a civil contract in that all rights and obligations must be stated in it. After the wedding no further arrangements can be made regarding the rights it has spelled out. This contract can stipulate that the wife has a right to demand a divorce if the husband marries again; or there can be a clause stipulating that the wife can demand a divorce, such as "You are divorced at any time, if you wish it." Today monogamous marriage is increasingly the norm (see Sura 4.3; 4.129), although many countries have not made a legal commitment to monogamy as the sole form. In the case of a divorce initiated by the husband, the contract is important; it determines what portion of the dowry is paid before the marriage and what portion upon divorce. Citizens of other countries need to be informed about these rules for the legal, economic, and social security of the wife. The care of the children must also be determined in such a case.

Normally the wife will share the home of her husband. In some cultures he can forbid her to leave the home or to receive visitors. In many Islamic countries the wife must have her husband's written permission to travel outside the country, especially if she wishes to travel with her children.

In Sunni inheritance law the Muslim husband cannot inherit from his Christian wife, nor can she inherit from her Muslim husband. In Shi'ite Islam (especially in Iran), Muslim children of a Christian mother have the right to inherit family possessions, but not Christian children. Christians can only inherit wealth or property if specific mention of them is made in the will or if they are given a specific monetary award or gift.

According to Islamic law, children fundamentally belong to their father. As long as the marriage exists, both parents have the right to care for the children, but if the father dies, his responsibilities normally transfer to the closest male relative. The mother has the right to care for young children. At the age of six for boys and eight for girls that right can cease, especially if she remarries. According to Islamic law for mixed marriages, this proviso that she raise the children becomes invalid if she as a divorced Christian leaves her husband's sphere of influence, that is, his country. Even in contemporary Turkey, small children are often left with their father according to Islamic practice.

## REMAINING TASKS AND OPPORTUNITIES

A Christian-Islamic marriage demands special effort from both partners to understand each other in their differences. These do not have to be burdens; they can be an enrichment. It is important that each makes an effort to intensively learn and understand the other's faith, culture (with its patterns of behavior), and ancestry. For even if the family of the Muslim partner has been living in another country for two or three generations, Muslims remain deeply influenced by many traditions of their homeland. Even if the Muslim partner was born in and is loyal to the same country as the non-Muslim partner, he or she is directed by faith toward the religious and cultural background of the Islamic countries. Still, in such marriages it is possible to respect the religious differences and to practice prayer together, for example at mealtime or free evening prayer.

It is important to understand such marriages in order to accept them. These marriages are opportunities for understanding, and their success helps bridge the gap between both faiths and cultures. They represent a special opportunity for Christian communities.

# 19

# The Bible and the Qur'an

On reading the Qur'an, Christians encounter stories, characters, events, and words that are familiar to them from the Old and New Testaments.

## PARALLELS IN THE QUR'AN TO THE OLD TESTAMENT

The proclamation concerning God, the Creator of the world and humanity, and God's representative in the world (the prophet himself) is the core of the message that Muhammad conveyed. As in the biblical creation stories, the Qur'an does not give details of the process of creation; the texts, which remind us of the Psalms, invite us to pray to the Creator and to be thankful and obedient in response to his good work.

> Glorify the name of thy Guardian-Lord Most High, Who hath created, and further, given order and proportion; Who hath ordained laws, and granted guidance. (Sura 87.1-3)

God created heaven and earth, plants, animals, angels, and spirits. The Qur'an tells us that Adam, the first human, was called into life by God as the highest and most beautiful creation, despite jealous opposition among the jinn (angel-like beings), and was destined to be the representative (caliph) of God on earth. The Qur'an describes the story of the creation of humanity and the opposition of the angels in this way:

> Behold, thy Lord said to the angels: "I will create a vice-regent on earth." They said: "Wilt Thou place therein one who will make mischief therein and shed blood?—Whilst we do celebrate Thy praises and glorify Thy holy (name)?" . . . And He taught Adam the names of all things; then He placed them before the angels, and said: "Tell Me the names of these if ye are right." They said: "Glory to Thee: of knowledge we have none, save what Thou hast taught us. . . . He said: "O Adam! tell them their names." . . . And behold, We said to the angels: "Bow down to Adam:" and they bowed down: Not so Iblis: he refused and was haughty: He was of those who reject Faith. . . . Then did Satan make them slip from the (Garden), and get them out of the state (of felicity) in which they had been. (Sura 2.30-36)

After the fall the first humans were banned from the garden. Yet Adam and Eve (her name is never given in the Qur'an) show remorse. The Qur'an then says: "But his Lord chose him (for His Grace): He turned to him, and gave him guidance" (Sura 20.122).

"Then learnt Adam from his Lord words of inspiration, and his Lord turned towards him; for He is Oft-Returning, Most Merciful" (Sura 2.37).

The Qur'an knows nothing about a continuing separation between God and humanity or of a profound guilt on the part of human beings. The human maintains dignity as a representative of God on earth.

The story is told of Adam's two sons in which the one whose sacrifice to God is not accepted kills his brother (Sura 5.27-32). The story of the flood and Noah is told again and again. After Adam, Noah is the first messenger and prophet of God: He calls, although unsuccessfully, for the rejection of false gods by the people of his day (Sura 71; 11.36ff.). Mention is made of the Tower of Babel, although in connection with stories of the pharaoh during the time of Moses (Sura 40.36-37).

Abraham plays an especially important role in the Qur'an. He is honored as a friend of God, as a model of faith, and a prophet of the one, true God. Like the Jewish extrabiblical tradition, the Qur'an also reports that Abraham recognized that God is more powerful than the stars. At first he holds the stars and moon to be gods, but then he sees that they set:

> When he saw the sun rising in splendour, he said: "This is my Lord; this is the greatest (of all)." But when the sun set, he said: "O my people! I am indeed free from your (guilt) of giving partners to Allah. For me, I have set my face, firmly and truly, towards Him Who created the heavens and the earth, and never shall I give partners to Allah." (Sura 6.78-79)

Islam calls the few who faithfully prayed to the one true God alone, yet who were neither Christians nor Jews (Sura 3.67) in the pre-Muslim era, *hanifs* or seekers.

When Abraham recognized God, he destroyed the idols of his father (Sura 21.51-70). The naming of Abraham's son and the story of his sacrifice are also told in the Qur'an (Sura 37.99-113). Most Muslim interpreters assume that Abraham's eldest son, Ishmael, not Isaac, was to be sacrificed. The Qur'an reports that Abraham and Ishmael, the progenitor of all Arabs, also revered as a prophet, founded the "House of God," the Kaaba, in Mecca (Sura 2.125). This tradition is unknown in the Bible. A long, beautiful sura tells of Joseph, the favorite son of Jacob (Sura 12). Moses takes up a lot of space in the Qur'an (he is mentioned in 36 suras). He is the man who talks with God (Sura 4.164). According to Islam he is the prophet and lawgiver of Israel. He brought the Holy Scripture of the Torah (*taurat*) to his people and liberated the Israelites from Egypt. He was at once a religious and political leader of his people, like Muhammad himself later. The conflicts between Moses and the pharaoh, the march of the Israelites through the (Red) Sea, and the drowning of the Egyptians in the sea are all told in the Qur'an. A passage analogous to the Ten Commandments is found in Sura 17.22-39. In the Qur'an, David is not only a king, but also a prophet who was to communicate the Holy Scripture of the Psalms (*zabur*). While the Bible knows also the dark sides of David's life, like adultery and murder, the Qur'an mentions only good things (Sura 38.21-25), as with all the prophets. This is because God chooses as messengers only the pious and good and it is not acceptable to assume that they commit major sins. Even more than about David, the Qur'an reports on his son, Solomon (Suleyman) and his great wisdom (Sura 21.78ff.).

## PARALLELS TO THE NEW TESTAMENT

Parallels in the New Testament are primarily in regard to John the Baptist (Yahya), Mary (Maryam), and Jesus (Isa). The announcement of the upcoming birth of John the Baptist to Zechariah (Zakariya) and his wife is portrayed similarly to the New Testament account. Other parallels to the New Testament concentrate on John the Baptist's prophetic work (compare Sura 3.38-41; 19.2-15; 21.90). Jesus is seen in the Qur'an as one of the great prophets and messengers of God who proclaimed the message of God's judgment prior to Muhammad. The virgin birth of Jesus is told, the miracles of Jesus are told or hinted at. As a prophet, Jesus had the task of calling the Israelites back to obedience to God and bringing the gospel as revealed Scripture to Christians. The Qur'an warns against seeing Jesus as more than a human, and disputes his death on the cross (compare Sura 4.157). The resurrection of Jesus is therefore not mentioned in the Qur'an.

## EXTRABIBLICAL CHRISTIAN PARALLELS
## TO THE QUR'AN

In the creation texts, in the Abraham tradition, in the Joseph sura, as well as in the Jesus stories of the Qur'an, it is evident that numerous details and interpretations do not find their parallels in the Old and New Testaments but in extrabiblical and postbiblical

Jewish and Christian traditions, the so-called apocryphal texts. Features are stressed in these texts that are similar to those in the Qur'an: the emphasis on the purity of Mary, the description of the birth of Jesus, the report of the miracle in which Jesus formed live birds out of clay, the emphasis on Jesus' prophetic task, and the little importance accorded to Jesus' death on the cross.

## BIBLICAL TRADITION WITHOUT PARALLELS IN THE QUR'AN

Thus, Christian and Jewish traditions that are not part of Christian Holy Scripture are suggested in the Qur'an. It cannot be overlooked, however, that most of the Bible has left no trace in the Qur'an. The books of the prophets in the Old Testament are unknown in the Qur'an, although Muhammad saw his assignment as similar to that of the biblical prophets. So the Qur'an knows nothing, for example, of Isaiah, Jeremiah, Amos, or Hosea.

According to the Qur'an, Holy Scripture is a collection only of revealed words of God. Therefore, even the Jesus tradition of the Qur'an recognizes only Jesus' preaching, that is, his spoken words, as Holy Scripture. For this reason there are no parallels in the Qur'an to the reports and texts of the early Christian community, as for example in Acts and the letters of the apostle Paul, and there is no indication that Muhammad ever encountered them.

## BIBLICAL TRADITION AND QUR'AN

For Muhammad, as for many Arabs of his time, most biblical stories and texts were probably only familiar as far as they were read in worship services or told among the people. It was hardly possible for the listeners to value and understand these stories in their biblical or historical perspective. Extrabiblical stories and traditions were also popular, especially among communities that had experienced Jewish and Christian influences. Thus, in the folk piety and in the worship of the Syrian-speaking church within the region

of the Arabs, a different image of the biblical tradition was transmitted than that of the official church teaching. This explains many
discrepancies between biblical and Qur'anic portrayals.

The Qur'an declares that these differences are due to the fact
that Holy Scripture of the Torah (*taurat*), the Psalms (*zabur*), and
the gospel (*injil*) were altered and adulterated through distortions
that have entered the texts during the course of the centuries.

> But because of their breach of their Covenant, We cursed them, and
> made their hearts grow hard: They change the words from their
> (right) places and forget a good part of the Message that was sent
> them. . . . From those, too, who call themselves Christians, We did
> take a Covenant, but they forgot a good part of the Message that
> was sent them. (Sura 5.13-14)

Since the Qur'an is understood as the conclusive revelation
that collects all earlier revelations and restores them, according to
Islamic conviction, Muslims use the Qur'an to demonstrate whether
a text in the Bible corresponds with the original revelation or not.

For Christians the canon (authoritative list of contents) of the
Holy Scripture was conclusively decided (at the latest) by the first
half of the fourth century. By the end of the second century, the
churches had already agreed on the major portions of the New
Testament canon. The oldest manuscripts demonstrate that the
ancient wording of the text was faithfully copied, though not without variant readings, from the earliest time. As the sacred Scriptures
for Christians, the Bible has through the course of history sustained
the church in the truth and been an unfailing source of intellectual
and spiritual power. This is so, for at its core stands Jesus Christ,
"the Word [become] flesh" (John 1:14). For Christians this confession makes the Bible the Word of God. The Bible is at the same
time a human word, because in it humans witness to Jesus Christ.
In its effects Christians see the continuing power of the resurrected
Christ through the Holy Spirit.

Islam has been shaped in decisive ways by Jewish and Christian biblical tradition. Yet one must not overlook the fact that in
key places the Qur'an has a different emphasis than the Bible. A
certain pattern is evident in the way the Qur'an presents biblical

stories. The Qur'an sees Muhammad's activity and experiences as prefigured in the biblical stories. Parallels are suggested: a people turning away from God, the sending to them of a prophet, rejection by the people of the proclamation brought to them. The repetition of this pattern repeatedly makes it clear that Muhammad is the "seal of the prophets" and brings the conclusive revelation.

Christians do not acknowledge the claim of Islam that the truth of biblical tradition should be judged by the Qur'an; for them, Jesus Christ is the measure of God's truth as the Holy Scripture confesses. Still, conversations between Christians and Muslims are necessary. Talking together reminds us of our common roots and helps to create mutual understanding, while at the same time making the limits of commonality clear.

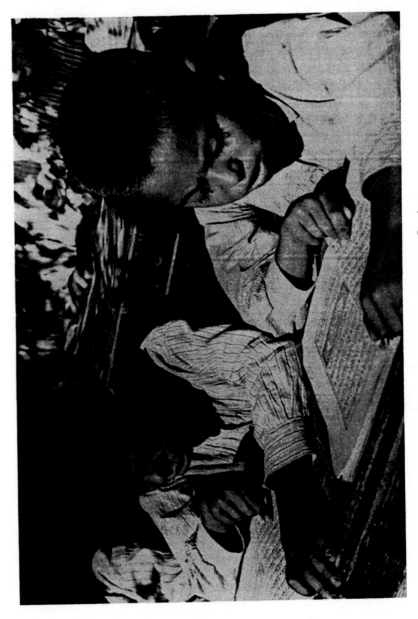

ARABIAN CHILDREN READING THE QUR'AN

# 20

## Jesus in Islam

Muslims venerate Jesus as one of the great prophets and messengers of God who, prior to Muhammad, already proclaimed the message of God's mercy, will, and judgment of humanity at the end of times. Muslims are not permitted to say anything dishonorable about Jesus or his mother, Mary. Should the name of Jesus or of another prophet be mentioned, then the pious Muslim adds the blessing, "Peace be with him."

In the Qur'an and in Islamic literature, the name of Jesus takes the form *Isa*. This form likely stems from Syrian, the language that many Christians in the Near East used at that time. Jesus is often named in the Qur'an with his title *al-masih*, the Messiah or Christ; but the Qur'an does not explain this title further. The New Testament gives Jesus the title "Messiah" ("Christ" in Greek), which means the anointed one of God, thereby taking up Old Testament tradition.

## THE BIRTH OF JESUS ACCORDING TO
## THE QUR'AN

The earliest mention of Jesus in the Qur'an is the account of his birth in Sura 19.16-33. This sura carries the name "Maryam." As in the Gospel of Luke, the story of John the Baptist's birth precedes that of Jesus. The Qur'an shares the Christian teaching that Mary was a virgin when she bore Jesus. The Qur'an, however, does not say that Jesus was conceived by the Holy Spirit, as the Apostles' Creed does. Rather it says that he was created in the womb of Mary by God through a word (compare Sura 21.91). Muslims agree that that word was *be* (Sura 3:47). God created Jesus as a sign of his mercy toward people of all the earth, for through Jesus' preaching many people were later to come to faith in the one God. After Jesus was born under a date palm, Mary returned to the city. There she was accused by her relatives of prostitution. At this point the infant child spoke up and explained that God had given him a "revelation" (a book) and had sent him to preach to the people as a prophet, and that he was to lead them to a common practice of prayer as well as to the giving of alms. He was, moreover, to honor and protect his mother. In referring to the miracle of the virgin birth, the Qur'an always calls Jesus "the son of Mary."

In this speaking miracle, Jesus described his later duties as those of a servant of Allah (*abd Allah*). The "revelation" or book refers to the gospel (*injil*). Muslims understand that a holy scripture or book (*kitab*) was revealed to Jesus, and thus Jesus was revealed as a prophet in the same way that the Qur'an reveals Muhammad as a prophet.

Already in this birth narrative, Jesus is seen as a creation of God like all people. In a later passage of the Qur'an, this becomes even clearer.

> She said: "Oh my Lord! How shall I have a son when no man hath touched me?" He said: "Even so: Allah createth what He willeth: when He hath decreed a plan, He but saith to it, 'Be,' and it is!" (Sura 3.47)

God demonstrated omnipotence by creating Jesus in the womb of Mary without a father's involvement. Even more miraculous, however, was the creation of Adam without father or mother; the same sura refers to this (Sura 3.59). Thus, the Qur'an warns against seeing Jesus as more than a human because of his unusual birth, such as seeing him as the "Son of God." The Qur'an emphasizes that Jesus also confesses God as his Lord and Creator.

## JESUS' DUTIES ACCORDING TO THE QUR'AN

The Qur'an sees the duties of Jesus, a prophet, primarily in calling the "children of Israel," who have fallen away from the teachings of Moses, back to obedience to God and his laws, that is, back to the Torah revealed by Moses. The Qur'an also mentions that Jesus partially lifted the strict food laws of the Old Testament (Sura 3.50; compare Sura 4.160).

Like other prophets, Jesus also received permission from God to do "signs" or miracles as proof of his divine assignment. In Sura 5.111-115 we are told that on Jesus' request God sent down a table with food from heaven. God thus confirmed his prophet and added this warning: "But if any of you after that resisteth faith, I will punish him with a penalty such as I have not inflicted on anyone among all the peoples" (Sura 5.115). Disbelief in the prophet is thus disbelief in God himself.

Jesus' healing the sick and raising the dead are also mentioned in the Qur'an, but without the details narrated in the Gospels (Sura 3.49; 5.110). Jesus is the only prophet of whom the Qur'an reports miracles of this kind. In Sura 61.6 a prophecy is mentioned that is unknown in Christianity, that after Jesus one more new prophet will appear whose name is *Ahmad*, "highly praised." This word is derived from the same root as "Muhammad." Based on such Qur'anic statements, Muslims believe Muhammad was mentioned in earlier Scriptures. Later Qur'an interpreters tried to connect this verse with Jesus' promise in the Gospel of John to send a "comforter," but the evangelist, John, linked this promise to the sending of the Holy Spirit (compare John 14:16; 15:26; 16:7).

The Qur'an also mentions that Jesus was exposed to particularly violent enemies and that God therefore strengthened him through the "Holy Spirit" (Sura 2.87; 5.110). According to the Qur'an, the "Holy Spirit" is created by God, is an angel, and is a prophet in his own right. His task is to deepen the knowledge of the faithful about the divine will for salvation and divine mercy so that they can prepare for the coming judgment without wavering, remaining steadfast under attack (Sura 58.22). For Jesus, the strengthening from the Spirit meant above all the obligation to carry out his duty to preach despite all opposition, as he had already done from the cradle (Sura 19.30).

When the Qur'an describes Jesus as "a Messenger of Allah, and His Word" (Sura 4.171) or "a Word from Him" (Sura 3.45), Christian readers may be reminded of the Gospel of John (chapter 1). But the Qur'an reads:

> O People of the Book! Commit no excesses. . . . Christ Jesus the son of Mary was (no more than) a Messenger of Allah, and His Word, which He bestowed on Mary, and a Spirit proceeding from Him. (Sura 4.171)

The word (*kalima*) is the creating word of God, through which Jesus was born. But according to the Qur'an, Jesus is not himself the Word of God as in the Gospel of John. When the Qur'an speaks of the Word (*kalam*) of God, which has existed since eternity, it refers to the heavenly original source from which all Holy Scriptures were revealed to the prophets.

Jesus' truthfulness and justice are demonstrated to the faithful in his model conduct of living. His peaceable disposition and gentleness (Sura 19.32) have an effect on people, spreading peace, well-being, and blessing throughout his community. No offense against God's law is reported of him. He belongs to those who stand especially close to God. With his calling, Jesus stands in the line of the great messengers of God like Adam, Noah, Abraham, Moses, and Muhammad.

## DEATH AND RESURRECTION OF JESUS
## ACCORDING TO THE QUR'AN

According to Islamic understanding, Jesus did not die on the cross. Following Muhammad's emigration from Mecca to Medina (the Hijra), some of the Jewish groups located there declared that they rejected him as a prophet because he was not of Jewish descent. In this argument, they referred to the fact that their ancestors had killed Jesus because they, likewise, could not accept his religious claim. The following Qur'an verse speaks to this situation:

> That they said (in boast), "We killed Christ Jesus the son of Mary, the Messenger of Allah"—but they killed him not, nor crucified him, but so it was made to appear to them, and those who differ therein are full of doubts, with no (certain) knowledge, but only conjecture to follow, for of a surety they killed him not—Nay, Allah raised him up unto Himself; and Allah is Exalted in Power, Wise. (Sura 4.157-158)

This was intended to show the Jews that their unfriendly intentions regarding Muhammad would be for naught, just as they had been at that time toward Jesus. Christian teachings about Jesus' dying for humanity's sins are also rejected by reference to this passage.

Still, it is difficult to understand the statement from verse 157, "but so it was made to appear to them." One view is that God gave another person—some commentators say Simon of Cyrene, others Judas Iscariot—the appearance of Jesus, so that the Jews believed him to be Jesus and crucified him, while the true Jesus was taken away. The Qur'an does not say exactly what happened.

## THE QUR'AN ON DIVINE SONSHIP
## AND THE TRINITY

Belief in the one and only God stands at the core of the teaching of the Qur'an and Muhammad. God tolerates no other gods beside him; he is one in his being (compare Sura 112). Those who view a creation as God's son, thereby honoring as divine something besides God, commit the inconceivable sin of "association" (*shirk*), for which there is no forgiveness. When Christians speak of Jesus as the "Son of God," Muslims understand this in terms of familial descent; they are reminded of ancient Arab concepts of families of gods (compare Sura 53.19ff.), against whom Muhammad directed his message (compare Sura 19.88-95).

Finally, the Qur'an accuses Christians of honoring Jesus as the "Son of God," while also honoring his mother Mary as the "Mother of God." The Qur'an sees this as further treason against the faith in the one God, as in fact faith in three gods (Father, Mother, Son). It makes a great effort to clear Jesus of the accusation that he had possibly evoked this heresy (Sura 5.116).

It is also the conviction of the Christian churches that faith in three gods is an aberration. But the fact that this rejection is expanded in the Qur'an to include the Christian belief in the Trinity (God in three persons) makes theological discussion difficult.

The Qur'an not only rejects the Trinity but also the central Christian confessions that are connected with the person of Jesus: "Nor can a bearer of burdens bear another's burden. If one heavily laden should call another to (bear) his load, not the least portion of it can be carried (by the other)" (Sura 35.18). Furthermore, the concepts and names for Jesus known in Christianity receive different meanings in the Qur'an, meanings that accord with Islamic teachings.

The Qur'an makes an effort to give Jesus a venerable place among the prophets and messengers of God, but it understands Jesus only as one of the messengers of God, merely human as all the others.


## JESUS IN THE UNDERSTANDING OF ISLAMIC THEOLOGY

Muslims warn against overestimating the role of Jesus for Islamic theology. The Qur'an's stories about Jesus and the later extra-Qur'anic stories are intended to strengthen piety. When Islamic theologians studied Jesus, they did so knowing that the Qur'an refutes the Christian confession of Jesus Christ as "true God and true human" and rejects the belief that his death atoned for sin. The Christian designation of Jesus as the "Son of God" in particular arouses opposition from Islamic theologians. Islamic theology makes a sharp distinction between the eternal and unchanging Creator and temporal creations, brought to life only through the power of the Creator. There is no room for the Christian conviction that God of God's own free choice became human, a creation.

Islamic theology rejects the Christian teaching that humans are entirely unable on their own to bring their relationship with God into a proper order. Muslims start by trying to do good and not fall into sin, and seek the help of God, who assists them. Because of this emphasis on human ability, on human choices and deeds in keeping the divine law, there is no need for atonement. For them Jesus' death can have no meaning for salvation, for establishing a right relationship between humanity and God. They find support for this view in Sura 4.175.

Still, Christians see no reason to doubt the historicity of Jesus' crucifixion, for not only the four evangelists report on it, but so also do other ancient non-Christian historians who gave this event no religious significance and who would therefore have no interest in inventing it.

Next to the doctrine of atonement through Christ's death on the cross, the belief in the Trinity has above all aroused opposition from Islamic scholars. The belief that the same God who has revealed himself in the Old Testament is revealed in Jesus Christ and in the power of the Holy Spirit is rejected by Islamic theology as irreconcilable with the confession of the unity of God (*tawhid*).

## JESUS IN ISLAMIC FOLK PIETY

While Islamic theologians were concerned with setting dogmatic boundaries between themselves and Christians when they spoke of Jesus, folk piety looked for elements that might serve spiritual edification. For the Islamic mystics or Sufis, Jesus has great importance. In him they see a great paradigm of a pious, humble, helping, and modest person. They may also see Muhammad that way, but as the "Seal of the Prophets," he had to be concerned with the legal and dogmatic, that is, external laws of Islamic community. For some of them, Jesus serves as the "Seal of Holiness," and he is one toward whom the pious can choose to orient their spiritual conduct.

The question of Jesus' death has led to various speculations in Muslim folk piety. If Jesus did not die on the cross, where and how did he die? Sura 4.158 reports that God "raised him up." But to where? Was Jesus, like Enoch (Idris), raised up alive into heaven (Sura 19.56-57; compare Gen. 5.24; Heb. 11:5)? Then he would have to return to earth again before the last judgment. For in Sura 19.33 the words of Jesus are reported: "So Peace is on me the day I was born, the day that I die, and the Day that I shall be raised up to life (again)!" The resurrection for all people can only take place on the last day, so his death must have taken place earlier. But the Qur'an gives no information about the time of Jesus' death.

Thus legends arose in Islamic tradition that were intended to give answers to these questions. According to one of these legends, Jesus was carried off by God shortly before the crucifixion to a safe place on earth. From there he wandered, preaching in Eastern countries, until his death. In Srinagar in Kashmir, a grave that is said to be his can be seen. A similar tradition was taken up at the end of the last century by Mirza Ghulam Ahmad, the founder of the Ahmadiyya movement. The Ahmadiyyas' account is that Jesus hung on the cross, went into a coma, was taken down and rubbed with an ointment, was healed, and traveled to Kashmir. Ahmad called on Muslims and Christians to wait no longer upon the return of Jesus, but to believe in him as the already appeared messianic preacher.

Other folk superstitions are that Jesus will come down alive from heaven before the last day. He will appear on a minaret of the Umayyad mosque in Damascus. After this, he will cause the Christians to recant their teaching of the Trinity, the killing of pigs (eating of pork is prohibited in Islam; also in Judaism), and will destroy the Antichrist (*dajjal*). Finally, he will marry. After he has unified Christians and Muslims into one people of God, he will die and be buried next to Muhammad in Medina.

Some of these legends are reflected in the so-called Gospel of Barnabas, a text written by a fourteenth-century monk in southern Italy who converted to Islam. In the form of a gospel, he wrote the life story of Jesus, in which he summarized the Islamic conceptions of Jesus and at the same time battled the Christian traditions where they conflicted with the Islamic. Thus, according to Islamic conviction, he lets Jesus prophesy the appearance of Muhammad and warns his community to follow this new prophet, whom he—in contradiction to the Qur'an—calls Messiah (compare Sura 61.6). This earlier Christ chose Barnabas as author because he had separated himself from Paul, supposedly because Paul was introducing into Christianity teachings that turned away from Jesus (compare Acts 15:36-40).


## HOW MODERN MUSLIM THEOLOGIANS SEE JESUS

Although the old disputes are far from settled, modern Muslim thinkers make an effort to find positive approaches for a dialogue with Christians about Christ.

One of the first contemporary reformers of Islamic thinking, the Egyptian Muhammed Abduh, went back to Mutazilite convictions, according to which the message of all prophets must be understandable to reason, because not only revelation but also reason has its source in God. All statements that conflict with reason rightly used are therefore unacceptable for faith. In connection with this, he questioned the New Testament miracle stories, because although miracle stories strengthen existing faith, they cannot arouse it, except perhaps superstitious faith. Faith is awakened by the reasonable preaching of the prophets (therefore, also by Jesus), who call for obedience to the one God in all realms of life and for the study of God's creation. Christians and Muslims could be united

into one religious community on the basis of the one divine "religion
of reason," to which Jews would also belong.

Abbas Mahmud Aqqad (1889–1964), one of the great Egyptian
critics of his time, tried to form an understanding of Jesus that
would recognize the distresses of Jesus' time and his attempt to
overcome them. At Jesus' time, almost the entire known world was
united in the Roman Empire. Jesus met the universal longing for
deliverance from the barbaric oppression of the Romans and for
lasting spiritual values with his proclamation of the universal love
of God for all people, especially the oppressed. For Aqqad, Muhammad's universal meaning is that he again communicated the
oneness of the only God for all people. Aqqad saw Jesus' universal
importance in his proclamation of the "religion of the love of God"
and equality of all people, thus refuting the idea that Jesus' effect
be limited to Israel.

The Egyptian doctor Muhammad Kamil Husayn (d. 1979) saw
the importance of Jesus' proclamation in that he called the individual to responsibility before God without compromise. The conscience is the word of God in a person and warns against doing
wrong or being silent regarding another's wrong. The conscience
calls the faithful to protest wrong and to come to the truth, and
keeps them from hiding silently in the anonymity of the masses
in order to avoid answering to God. A just society is possible only
if each person sees and freely develops responsibility for justice
and truth. However, the political and religious leaders of society
valued Jesus' proclamation as otherworldly, wishful thinking. According to them, people need strong leadership that controls society
and determines public opinion. Individual criticism from the conscience would weaken society. Thus, Husayn saw the events on
Good Friday in Jerusalem, the high priests and the Roman military,
that is, the religious and secular leaders, agreed to kill Jesus in the
interests of peace and order. Though Jesus was not killed, at least
not by the Jews, nevertheless, by simply intending the death of
Jesus, who was God's prophet, the religious leaders crucified their
own conscience, which is to be oriented toward God and God's
will alone, and with it destroyed "true religion." The powerful try

repeatedly to destroy conscience, resulting in endless injustice and suffering to the present day.

Besides these voices who are striving for dialogue between Christians and Muslims, there are also those who see in Christianity only the falling away from the teachings of the prophet Isa (Jesus). For Muhammad Rashid Rida (1865–1935), the flawed sense of justice on the part of Christians is made apparent in that the individual is not responsible for his or her own failings, but that Jesus, as the innocent one, must bear the punishment resulting from injustices wrought by others. In order to justify his criticism of the history of Christianity and its involvement with unjust state power, such as in the Crusades or colonialism, Rida points to Jesus' own words, that his kingdom is not of this world (compare John 18:36). Rida also holds that Muhammad was the first statesman legitimized by God; for this reason law and justice are guaranteed only in his community. Fundamentalistic teachers like the Pakistani Abu ala Mawdudi thus support their opinion that Christian minorities in Islamic countries will be granted the "protection" of Muslims, but should not have any decision-making power in matters of the government.

## PART FIVE

# Islam—A Christian Appreciation

This last part includes an effort to appreciate Islam from the Christian perspective and to evaluate it. Here we do not make an attempt—as in the preceding four parts—to give objective information as much as possible. In the evaluation our own perspective will be expressed.

# 21

## The Witness of Faith

Neither Christians nor Muslims can be silent about the center of their faith: They must pass on what has become the core of their life. For Christians the gift, the call of Jesus Christ, is their assignment; for Muslims it is the *dawah*, the invitation to faith. This chapter will discuss both.

### THE OBLIGATION TO WITNESS

The first fundamental rule of the practice of Islam, the *shahadah*, obligates the Muslim to pray before God and to confess in conversation with other people: "I confess that there is no God but Allah. I confess that Muhammad is the prophet." The Qur'an itself demands of each Muslim: "Invite (all) to the Way of thy Lord with wisdom and beautiful preaching; and argue with them in ways that are best and most gracious" (Sura 16.125). *Dawah* in Islam is understood as an invitation to faith. Others are invited to become Muslim, for Muslims are "the best of Peoples, evolved for mankind, enjoining what is right, forbidding what is wrong, and believing in Allah" (Sura 3.110). But all recruitment is to take place without the use of force. "Let there be no compulsion in religion" (Sura 2.256).

For us Christians it is the same: "We cannot keep from speaking about what we have seen and heard" (Acts 4:20). We cannot avoid it because Jesus Christ himself gave us the task: "You will be my witnesses in Jerusalem, in all Judea and Samaria, and to the ends of the earth" (Acts 1:8). This witness is to reach all people, including Muslims. For Christians believe that God revealed God's innermost self in Christ Jesus: "For in him the whole fullness of deity dwells bodily" (Col. 2:9). The Christian witness to others should include no pressure or force; this would contradict the love of Christ. Where Christians have behaved differently, such as in the time of colonial expansion by the so-called Christian nations of the West, or where they still discriminate against Muslims, this takes place in contradiction to the gospel of Christ. Not disdain toward others but love shall determine the actions of the witnesses of Jesus Christ. Jesus himself said: "As the Father has sent me, so I send you" (John 20:21). Christian mission, accordingly, is to enter into this sending, witnessing that the fullness of God has appeared in Christ Jesus and convincing others by words and deeds of love. It is this to which we are called at the end of the Gospel of Matthew (Matt. 28:19-20), to go and make disciples of all nations.

## ON LISTENING TO ONE ANOTHER

The encounter between Christians and Muslims cannot exclude the prerequisite to listen when openness is the desire and the goal is to understand one another and learn from one another. Both sides, Christians and Muslims, must recognize that the faith witness of both partners is authentic and that the unique experiences, convictions, and behaviors of each should be discussed. Only if both sides strive to accept the other's faith witness can the first discovery of commonality take place. This acceptance can prevent giving up the encounter in resignation when differences come to the fore.

Thus it is a problem for Christians that, according to strict Islamic teaching, conversion from Islam to another faith, including Christianity, is seen as "falling away from God," punishable by death. Although this penalty is rarely carried out today, Muslims must still reckon with considerable pressure from family and society if they wish to become Christians. To be sure, there would also be considerable conflict in a Christian family if a member wished to convert to Islam, yet the recognition of the individual conscience—at least in the Western world—has become widely accepted.

In this connection the Christian-Islamic consultation in 1976 in Chambesy, Switzerland (near Geneva), should be mentioned. There the Christian and Muslim participants expressly emphasized and recognized the basis of religious freedom, "that Muslims as well as Christians must have full freedom to convince and to be convinced and to live their faith."

On the Islamic side it should be asked again what it means that Muhammad saw Jews and Christians as communities with which Muslims could enter into contract and what "respected them as partners" means. Even the Qur'an speaks of the three faith communities of the people of the book, *ahl al-Kitab*, as of equal value. God gave each of them its own way and its own order, *shirat*, and delays judgment until the last day. The three religions are supposed to compete for the good and each to strive in faithfulness to its own tradition (compare Sura 5.48-49; also see pp. 125–26 above). Thus Christians, together with Jews and Sabaeans, are expressly assured that "on them shall be no fear, nor shall they grieve" on the last day if they believe in Allah and the last day and do right (Sura 5.69).

On the Christian side it should be remembered that Jesus behaved differently with people of other faiths, such as with Samaritans, than was common at the time among Jews. In their eyes the Samaritans, who were related to them in faith, were "half-heathens" whom they disdained. Jesus did not accept the Jews' rejection of the Samaritans, but consciously chose examples from among them when he wanted to represent a model practice of faith. Cases in point are the story of the good Samaritan (Luke 10:25-35) and of the outcast leper who was the only one among ten who were healed who returned to thank the Lord (Luke 17:16).

Jesus' example should lead Christians to respectfully encounter the daily practice of faith with which Muslims honor God. For one can appreciate how for Muslims the binding rules from the Qur'an and the *hadith* (the teachings of Muhammad) shape the way they live. At the same time the faith tradition of Christians can gain renewed importance: that God does not abandon humans to their errors and failures but forgives them for the sake of Jesus Christ and through him always gives a new beginning in obedience to God's will.

By listening to one another and through mutual respect, open encounter is possible between Christians and Muslims. This respect includes openness to each other's witness of faith.


## ISLAMIC PREJUDICES AGAINST CHRISTIAN FAITH

According to Islamic perspective, nothing distinguishes Christians and Muslims more decisively than the different understandings of the person of Jesus and the Christian doctrine of the Trinity. For Muslims, the confession of the oneness of God, *tawhid*, renders impossible the recognition of Jesus Christ, the son of Mary, as the son of God. According to the Qur'an, while they can identify him as belonging to "(the company of) those nearest to Allah" (Sura 3.45) and even as "a Sign unto men and a Mercy from Us" (Sura 19.21) "for all peoples" (Sura 21.91), Jesus still remains the next to the last in the line of messengers and prophets, merely human like all of them.

Christians are unable to retreat from the witness of the New Testament. According to its testimony Jesus Christ is more than a prophet whose duty is fulfilled, as with all the prophets in the Qur'an, as a preacher of repentance calling people to the service of God (compare Sura 3.51). Christians see that in him "the tender mercy of our God" (Luke 1:78) takes on human flesh and blood. Therefore God's "tender mercy" shines through his deeds. He did not overlook the sick and the blind. He excluded none on the fringes of society. He chose his disciples from among despised country folk and tax collectors, against whom society discriminated. Even more, he assumed the authority of God in forgiving sins. So he spoke a direct and authoritative word of forgiveness to a woman caught committing adultery (John 8:1-11) and to the paralytic (Mark 2:9-10). Even more important, Jesus' life and death became the measure of God's love. When reviled he did not revile (1 Pet. 2:23); as he loved his enemies so he summoned his disciples to love their enemies (Matt. 5:44); upon the cross he died with the word of forgiveness on his lips (Luke 23:34), holding fast to love until the end (Phil. 2:5-8). Not only was his will subject to the will of God even unto death ("Father . . . not what I will, but what thou wilt," Mark 14:36 RSV), but his will was one with God's will. He himself bore witness: "The Father and I are one" (John 10:30). In Jesus, and in his relation with the Father, we see the identity of God.

Muslims fear that the designation of Jesus as the Son of God contradicts the oneness of God, and that Jesus becomes for Christians a God in addition to the one God. But the very reason Christians designate Jesus as the Son of God is to make clear that Jesus is indissolubly one with God, not a second god or an addition. For them God confirmed this unity by the resurrection of Jesus from the dead.

Muslims have similar difficulties with the Christian understanding of the Trinity as well. It is important to remember that Arabic has no word for "three-in-one" or "threefold," but only for "threeness," *tathlith*. This language difficulty alone creates a misunderstanding of the Trinity as a threeness of gods. Accordingly the Qur'an warns: "Say not 'Trinity': desist. . . . For Allah is One God" (Sura 4.171), and according to another passage from the Qur'an Jesus warns against taking him and his mother Mary "as gods in derogation of Allah" (Sura 5.116).

With the oneness of God, Muslims see God's incomparability both threatened and violated when God is compared with a human who begets a son by Mary. That would make him a God-Father, Mary a God-Mother, and Jesus a God-Son. Christians often do not realize that the Qur'an is defending against heathen notions in its words about the Trinity, words that Christians consider strange and inappropriate. For Christians, however, it is precisely in God's triunity that one sees God's incomparability. God as love is not a simple unity but a complex unity of relations. It is of the revelation of this kind of eternal, divine, and enduring love between Jesus and the Father and between God and us that Christians speak when they confess the triune God. The God who creates is at the same time the God who is present as the rejected and crucified one in creation, and at the same time the God who unites all in love through the Holy Spirit. It is of this love that the Holy Spirit bears witness as the Spirit summons people to follow Christ and leads them to faith and trust in the one triune God.

## COMPLETE WITNESS

"Faith by itself, if it has no works, is dead" (James 2:17). Faith is only convincing when it is reflected in daily activities and trustworthiness and takes shape in practical life. Christians in this regard are frequently impressed by Muslims when they see their way of living. And Muslims also take notice when they see that Jesus' love motivates Christian actions in daily living even in the absence of a multitude of words.

In this respect Muslims have high expectations of Christians. The Qur'an speaks of Christians being the people nearest in love to Muslims, because they are dedicated to God and "are not arrogant" (Sura 5.82). Another passage says that God "sent after them Jesus the son of Mary, and bestowed on him the Gospel; and We ordained in the hearts of those who followed him Compassion and Mercy" (Sura 57.27).

The earliest Islamic community in Mecca experienced a demonstration of Christian love: When they were persecuted some of their followers found asylum with a Christian emperor in Ethiopia. Some Muslims carried this expectation of acceptance over to their contemporary quest for asylum and work in various countries of the West such as Germany or the United States, because they hoped to come to places still shaped by Christian values. Muslims therefore expect to be fully accepted in society and respected as neighbors, as well as to receive the necessary freedom to practice their faith. In return they often refer to Muslim countries that gave protection and freedom to Jews and Christians. Should not Christians today be prepared to take similar steps by clearly supporting a plural cultural existence? Should they not help Muslims become integrated without pressures to conform? Many Western countries have become permanent homes for most of those who have come, rather than guest countries.

Such expectations are justified. Still, Muslims must also ask themselves what they will do so that Christians and members of other non-Islamic faiths can correspondingly live in Islamic countries with equal rights and practice their faith without restriction.

Christians and Muslims can give a concrete and visible witness to their faith if they live with one another as good neighbors. Hospitality and neighborliness have been high values in Islam as well as in Christianity. They should also help determine the shape of encounters and relations between Christian and Muslim communities in the same town, so that Muslims and Christians can live together peacefully.

# 22

# A Christian Evaluation
## of Islam

## PARTNERS IN FAITH DIALOGUE

Contacts with Muslim people and groups have become everyday experiences in many European countries and are increasingly common in North America. For countries like Germany, the native population still has a tendency to judge adherence to Islam as simply an extreme aspect of the "foreigner problem." They think that Muslims are "foreigners" who behave differently and do not actually belong. One can weigh this difference from societal, political, and cultural standpoints. Yet Islam is above all a religious reality for Muslim people, one that fundamentally shapes their personal and community life.

Thus the first step to an evaluation is understanding: Islam is an authentic faith that shapes our Muslim neighbors' innermost being and determines their attitudes in life. And the Islamic faith is generally more tradition oriented than the recent Western shape of Christian faith, which has experienced considerable secularization. With Islam a faith has arisen in western European society that is growing and brings a permanent change to the entire religious situation. Nonetheless, Islam in many countries still lacks a common institutional shape that would make it clearly and legally a "religious community." Yet we are only fair to the Islamic population when we understand them from their religious core and respect them as a faith community. Muslims have become important partners in faith conversation.

## A DIFFERENT REVELATION?

"I confess that there is no God but Allah. I confess that Muhammad is his prophet." In this central confession the two fundamental experiences of Islamic faith are expressed: the oneness and majesty of God which overwhelms people and leads them to worship and obedience, as well as the mercy of God in showing people the right way to salvation in the word of the Qur'an as revealed by the prophet. In both experiences Muslims see themselves in the tradition of biblical revelation. It is beyond question for them that it is the same God to whom both Christians and Muslims pray. According to Islamic conviction, however, Christians have offended the oneness of God through their false teachings about Jesus Christ and the Trinity. That is why Muslims believe that only the Qur'an with its emphasis on the oneness of God can be the guide to the truth of revelation.

An evaluation from the Christian perspective must also look at the closeness of both faiths. It is not easy to see similarities after centuries of discussion in which the differences have almost always been emphasized. Yet the Islamic confession of the one God is virtually no different from the biblical commandment, "I am the LORD your God . . . you shall have no other gods before me" (Exod. 20:2). This similarity is evidence of the fact that Christianity and Islam—together with Judaism—stand in the same faith tradition. Therefore Christians and Muslims have many commonalities in central questions of faith and life: thankfulness for creation and responsibility for its preservation, security through faith in God, expectation of the judgment of human deeds, criticism of the idolatry of earthly goals and goods, commitment to justice and peace, and solidarity with the weak.

How can this inner relationship between Christianity and Islam be evaluated? Islam claims that the Qur'an is the only valid standard because it is the "last" revelation and Muhammad is the "Seal of the Prophets." Christians, in contrast, believe God revealed Godself in Jesus Christ once and for all and therefore any later proclamation must be related to this event. So according to Christian understanding there can be no bearer of revelation who makes Jesus Christ obsolete. This does not reduce Muhammad's quality as a prophetic preacher who called for a return to the one God. This Christian evaluation of Muhammad and his proclamation, however, cannot satisfy Muslims because they see him as the final revelation.

## A WAY TO SALVATION?

Christian faith also begins and ends with worship of the one God and God's majesty. In the sending of Jesus Christ, his preaching and healing, his crucifixion and resurrection, Christians experience the truth and reality of God: that God cares for humanity and all of creation. God's rule is the rule of love. In the story of Jesus Christ Christians experience at the same time their own truth and reality: that they are "good" because in the death and resurrection of Jesus Christ they are given new life, even though they repeatedly experience the brokenness and sin of their own being and cannot overcome their sinfulness in their own strength.

Jesus is not unknown in Islam: He is revered as a prophet and messenger of God. But Jesus is, according to Christian understanding, misunderstood in Islam because he is seen "only" as a prophet, and certainly not as a crucified and raised prophet. Christians confess Jesus Christ as the "Son of God." It is a misunderstanding to think that Christians are elevating a creation, a human being, to a place of divine honor next to God. In truth they believe that they thus experience Godself in Jesus Christ and his healing love. God became flesh, not flesh becomes God. It is this fundamental experience of Christian faith that the church has expressed in confession of the "triunity" of God: God is present in the midst of our world as the Son who prays to the Father, and through this crucified and risen one, the Spirit of love summons all people to faith in God.

Thus the real and decisive difference between Christianity and Islam comes to the fore, a difference which a Christian evaluation, with all due respect to the Islamic faith, must describe clearly: that God came down into the midst of our human world and that God became subject to suffering and death because the divine love drives God to be present with and redeem a lost creation. This understanding of divine vulnerability is foreign to Islam.

Is Islam then just as legitimate a way to salvation, despite being clearly different from the Christian faith, inasmuch as it is directed toward the same goal—the one God? For Muslims the answer to this question lies in their obedience to God's law. God has prescribed clear obligations and rules that are intended to help them live their entire lives before God in human society: the law, sharia, God's good order for the faithful. In obedience to God's law they experience salvation and find security in looking toward God's judgment and eternity.

Islam sees humans quite honestly with all their weaknesses and temptations to evil, but in the end it is optimistic about them. People are of course created good by God. Therefore they are capable of doing good and finding the right way to salvation through serving God. God in God's mercy can forgive evil deeds if people are penitent.

Christian faith agrees that humans will the good; but it also knows that despite their best intentions humans continually fail to do the good. The Christian experience of brokenness and guilt is dogmatically called "original sin." That is to say, the human failure to submit to God's complete lordship in life, disclosed most clearly in the human rejection of Jesus on the cross, permeates our existence and corrupts our societies. But the God whom we rejected, in undeserved love lifts us up and heals our disobedience. For Christians salvation is bound to God's love which took shape in

Jesus Christ. There is no other God than the God of such love; and there is no other salvation outside this love, for this love is our salvation. Indeed, to know God in God's supreme manifestation of self-giving love is to know God differently than apart from this. Nevertheless, the faith has and must always confess: Humans cannot determine the boundaries of God's love.

## POLITICS FOR GOD?

To many people today Islam no longer seems like a religion, but like a political force.

Ever since the prophet Muhammad brought into being the first Islamic community in the second half of his ministry in Medina, the political dimension has been part of Islam. It has given Islam an inherent tendency to take a political shape. This is a fundamental difference from much of present-day Christianity, which often has not included government and politics in its thought and deeds. Christians remember the words of Jesus: "My kingdom is not from this world" (John 18:36). This distancing is repeated in a different form in Western-Christian self-understanding in the separation of church and state. This makes it difficult for Christians to understand and value the political starting point of Islam, especially because it expresses itself very aggressively in some regions of the Islamic world.

At the same time this starting point is appropriate. God created the world and gave appropriate laws for nature and humanity. It is the mission of the faithful to shape not only their own lives, but the entire world according to God's will and thus to fulfil their destiny, namely to be an echo and mirror of God's justice and wisdom. This goal includes all of human life—including the political, social, and legal realms.

In this connection the question of force is decisive. Islam accuses Christianity, which is often apolitical, of leaving the governmental realm to itself, that is to uncontrolled human egotism and power struggles. Islam in contrast has subjected the use of state power to the law of God. A Christian evaluation must respect the goal of Islam and also hear the critical questions put to the Christian position. Yet Christians have their own critical questions to ask of Islam.

The first question is this: Is there not a danger that religion can be misused and made into a shield for human interests? Religion has power over hearts, and the hope to establish an earthly kingdom of justice and peace can motivate people. The Bible is skeptical regarding such utopian expectations because it acknowledges the weakness of human nature and our susceptibility to temptation. The history of Islamic governments shows that many of their leaders carried out generally pragmatic politics without particularly lofty religious ideals. There are also instances when Islamic religion is distorted into a total ideology and is made to serve transparent power interests. Then Islam can become destructive "in the name of God," just as Christianity has at times, rather than create peace.

The second question is related to the first. If Islamic law represents the will of the one God for the world, then how can there be room in this world for those who think and believe differently? Every universal religion, and especially the monotheistic revelatory religions which include both Christianity and Islam, carry with their claim to truth such an undercurrent of exclusivity. That is appropriate as long as the battle for truth is fought with intellectual and spiritual powers.

Today the question is asked thus: Will Islam be able to find its place in the modern world, to really recognize its political and spiritual plurality, and to practice the tolerance for others that it demands for itself, including the right for Christians to become Muslims and Muslims Christian? Asked differently, can Islam accept non-Islamic minorities within its realm of power as citizens with equal rights and guarantee them protection and freedom, including the freedom to propagate, within the framework of generally recognized human rights?

## ENCOUNTER

Closeness and distance at the same time characterize the inner relationship between the Christian and Islamic faiths. The varied history of relations between Muslims and Christians corresponds to this. Today the situation has reached a new phase, at least for Europe and North America: Christians and Muslims live close together and have a new opportunity for encounter.

Despite their differences in belief and practice, some questions for conversations between Christians and Muslims can be formulated that expand on the starting points already mentioned:

- What responsibilities do Christians and Muslims have in regard to the created world that has been entrusted to human beings to protect its many resources and numerous animals and plants?
- What meaning does the quest for God's justice have in a world that is so full of injustice?
- What can we learn from each other's self-understanding about our religions? What are some of our common beliefs, ways of living, and concerns?
- In what ways can a faith orientation focused on mysticism and the inner life bring Christians and Muslims closer together?
- How can Christians and Muslims work together to enhance human life and to contribute to peace and harmony in the world?

# Appendices

# Chronology

## DATES FROM ISLAMIC HISTORY

| | |
|---|---|
| 4th–6th cent. A.D. | Arabian Peninsula in tension between Byzantium and Persia |
| ca. 570 | Birth of Muhammad in Mecca |
| 622 | Hijra, Muhammad's emigration to Medina |
| 630 | Conquest of Mecca |
| 632 | Muhammad's death |
| 632–634 | Caliph Abu Bakr |
| 634–644 | Caliph Umar |
| 634–644 | Conquest of Egypt, Palestine, Syria, Mesopotamia, and Persia |
| 635 | Conquest of Damascus |
| 636 | Defeat of the Persians and Byzantines |
| 644–656 | Caliph Uthman |
| ca. 653 | Final edition of the Qur'an |
| 656–661 | Caliph Ali |
| 661–750 | Caliphate of the Umayyad dynasty; Damascus becomes the capital |

| | |
|---|---|
| 680 | Death of Husayn at Kerbala |
| 691 | Construction of the Dome of the Rock on the temple mount in Jerusalem |
| 711 | Muslim armies enter Spain |
| 715 | Muslim armies conquer Kashgar (in Chinese Turkestan) |
| 732 | Battle of Tours (or Poitiers) victory of Charles Martel |
| 749–1258 | Caliphate of the Abbasid dynasty headquartered in Baghdad |
| 870 | Death of Bukhari, collector of the most respected *hadith* corpus |
| 909 | Beginning of Fatimid rule in North Africa |
| 922 | Al-Hallaj, a Sufi (mystic), executed for blasphemy |
| 935–939 | Attack and conquest of Genoa |
| 972 | Founding of Al-Azhar University in Cairo |
| 1036 | Death of Avicenna (Ibn Sina) |
| 1099 | Crusaders conquer Jerusalem |
| 1111 | Death of Al-Ghazzali |
| 1166 | Death of al-Jilani, founder of first Sufi brotherhood |
| 1187 | Saladin (Salah ad-Din) regains Jerusalem |
| 1196 | Establishment of a Sultanate in Delhi (India) |
| 1198 | Death of Averroes (Ibn Rushd) |
| 1204 | Conquest of the Mongols into Russia, Silesia, Anatolia, Persia, and India |
| 1236 | The fall of Cordoba through Ferdinand III |
| ca. 1300 | Marco Polo reports of Muslims in Yünnan and in the Chinese harbor cities |
| 1258 | Fall of Baghdad; end of Abbasids |
| after 1301 | Ascent of the Ottomans (Turks) |
| 1453 | Mehmed II (Fatih) conquers Constantinople |
| 1492 | Conquering of Granada, capital of the last Arab emirate in Spain |
| 1517 | Ottomans unify the Near Eastern Muslim lands |

| | |
|---|---|
| 1520–1566 | Suleyman the Magnificent (Ottoman ruler) |
| 1526 | Ottomans conquer Hungary |
| 1529 | First siege of Vienna fails |
| after 1556 | Government of Akbar, Moghul kingdom in India (decay after 1707) |
| after 1600 | First Muslim state in the Indonesian islands |
| 1683 | Second siege of Vienna fails, beginning of the decline of the Ottoman Empire |
| 1773 | The British East India Company becomes an official government board of British rule in India |
| 1798–1801 | Napoleon's campaign to Egypt |
| 19th century | Permeation and division of the Maghreb of the Near and Middle East by the colonial powers of France and England |
| 1803–1818 | First rule of the Wahhabites in Arabia |
| 1803 | Last region in India under Moghul rule comes under British control |
| after 1849 | Second rule of the Wahhabites in Arabia |
| 1858 | India becomes a British crown colony (Government of India Act of 1858) |
| 1881–1885 | Mahdi rebellion in Sudan |
| 1914 | Ottoman Empire joins the side of the central powers in World War I |
| 1917 | Balfour Declaration |
| 1923 | Proclamation of the Turkish Republic |
| 1928 | Foundation of the Muslim Brotherhood |
| 1945 | Proclamation of the Indonesian Republic |
| 1946 | Jordan, Lebanon, Syria are recognized as independent |
| 1947 | Foundation of Pakistan (separation from India) |
| 1948 | Proclamation of the State of Israel |
| 1954–1962 | Algerian war of independence from France |
| 1962 | Foundation of the Muslim World League |
| 1967 | Six-Day War in the Near East |
| after 1972 | Foundation of the Islamic Conference |

| 1973 | Yom Kippur War |
| 1979 | Proclamation of the Islamic Republic of Iran |
| 1991 | Gulf War |
| 1993 | Peace accord between Israel and the Palestine Liberation Organization (PLO) |

## COMPARISON DATES FROM WESTERN HISTORY

| A.D. 476 | "Fall" of Rome |
| after 565 | Irish-Scottish and Anglo-Saxon mission in Germany |
| 590–604 | Pope Gregory I (the Great) |
| 719–754 | Boniface as a missionary in Germany |
| 749 | Death of John of Damascus, who defined theological relation of Islam and Christianity |
| 768–814 | Reign of Charlemagne |
| 800 | Crowning of the Holy Roman Emperor, Charlemagne |
| 843 | Division of the empire, prefiguring modern Europe |
| 910 | Cluny founded |
| 936–973 | Otto I (the Great) |
| 1054 | Schism between East and West in Christendom |
| 1071 | Normans seize Sicily |
| 1096–1099 | First Crusade |
| 1122 | Concordat of Worms: end of investiture controversy |
| 1147–1149 | Second Crusade |
| 1152–1190 | Frederick I Barbarossa |
| 1189–1193 | Third Crusade |
| 1198–1216 | Pope Innocent III |
| 1209 | Beginning of Francis of Assisi's ministry |
| 1215 | Fourth Lateran Council; Magna Carta in England |

| | |
|---|---|
| 1232 | Inquisition established |
| 1274 | Death of Thomas Aquinas, end of high scholasticism |
| 1294 | Death of Roger Bacon |
| 1309–1377 | Popes in Avignon ("Babylonian Captivity") |
| 1378–1417 | The Great Schism |
| 1414–1418 | Council of Constance; Jan Hus burned at stake |
| 1453 | Fall of Constantinople |
| 1464 | Death of Nicholas of Cusa |
| 1492 | Columbus discovers America |
| 1517 | Martin Luther posts the 95 theses |
| 1519–1555 | Charles V |
| 1524–1525 | Peasants' War |
| 1540 | Society of Jesus founded |
| 1545–1563 | Council of Trent |
| 1555 | Peace of Augsburg |
| 1598 | Edict of Nantes (lifted 1685) |
| 1618–1648 | Thirty Years War |
| 1701 | Society for the Propagation of the Gospel in Foreign Parts founded |
| 1703–1791 | John Wesley |
| 1740–1786 | Frederick II of Prussia |
| 1761–1834 | William Carey |
| 1776 | American Declaration of Independence |
| 1789 | French Revolution |
| 1806 | End of the Holy Roman Empire |
| 1859 | Start of the building of the Suez Canal |
| 1862–1890 | Bismarck as Prussian Prime Minister |
| 1864 | Pius IX, Syllabus of Errors |
| 1870 | Pius IX, Vatican I, Pope stated to be infallible |
| 1910 | Edinburgh World Mission Conference |
| 1914–1918 | World War I |
| 1917 | Russian October Revolution (Bolshevik Revolution) |
| 1933–1945 | National Socialist regime in Germany |

| | |
|---|---|
| 1939–1945 | World War II |
| 1948 | World Council of Churches organized, Amsterdam |
| 1950–1953 | Korean War |
| 1952 | Explosion of the first American H-bomb |
| 1957–1975 | Vietnam War |
| 1962 | John XXIII, Vatican II; Cuban Missile Crisis |
| 1968 | The "Prague Spring" is crushed |
| 1989 | Fall of the Berlin Wall |

# Islamic and Christian Holiday Calendar

## 1. ISLAMIC HOLIDAYS

*Ramadan:* designation of the month of fasting. Muhammad received the revelation during this period. From dawn until sunset faithful Muslims refrain from eating, drinking, smoking, and sexual intercourse. After sunset families and neighbors gather for communal eating.

*Night of Power* (also called Night of Destiny), *Laylat al-Qadr:* one of the five holy nights (27th night in the month of fasting); remembrance of the revelation of the first five verses of Qur'an Sura 96 to Muhammad.

*Festival of Breaking the Fast, Id-al-Fitr,* also called "small festival": conclusion of the month of fasting.

*Festival of Sacrifice, Id-al-Adha:* Highest holiday in Islam. For most Muslims, a remembrance of Abraham's expected sacrifice of his son, Ishmael. Families slaughter a sacrificial animal, usually a sheep.

_New Year:_ The Islamic lunar year begins with the remembrance of the emigration from Mecca in 622. Because of its dependence on the lunar cycle, the Islamic year is about eleven days shorter than the Western-Gregorian. Thus, New Year's Day is set anew each year.

_Ashura:_ The tenth day of the first Islamic month. On this day, Noah is said to have debarked from the ark. In the Shi'ite tradition one remembers the murder of Husayn on this day, and for this reason it is a day of fasting.

_Mawlid:_ One of the five holy nights; birthday of the prophet.

Because the lunar calendar is the foundation for determining the dates of Islamic holidays, the dates change each year. According to traditional Islamic understanding, the dates of the beginnings of the months may not be calculated mathematically, but are to be determined only by observation (first appearance of the increasing crescent moon) and proclaimed after this. This leads to Islamic holidays being celebrated on varying dates in different countries: a difference of one to two days is possible.

The primary holidays, lasting several days, are the Festival of Breaking the Fast and the Festival of Sacrifice. These are also official holidays in Islamic countries. The five "holy nights" do not interfere with public work life, being matters more of folk piety.

## 2. MOVABLE CHRISTIAN HOLIDAYS

The dates of holidays of Christianity are fixed differently among the various church families. This is partially due to the fact that not all churches use the fixed calculations resulting from the calendar reform of Pope Gregory VIII (1582); some begin from a different starting date. In the following pages, the fixed dates for the Western (Evangelical and Catholic) are listed beside the dates for the Eastern churches. This difference is quite substantial. It does not take into account that the Greek Orthodox Church (as does the Syrian Orthodox Church) celebrates Christmas on the 25th of December (not listed here because it is not a movable holiday), while the Russian Orthodox Church celebrates it on the 7th of January. The Armenian church (including Armenian Protestant) celebrates on January 6, although this has nothing to do with calendar differences; it is a fundamentally different dating. The Armenian church follows the Western churches in the date of Easter and the holidays related to it.

## 3. CALENDARS

| | | |
|---|---|---|
| 1994 | February 12 | Beginning of Ramadan |
| | March 9-10 | Night of Power |
| | March 13 | Festival of Breaking the Fast |
| | April 3 | Easter (Western) |
| | May 1 | Easter (Eastern) |
| | May 21 | Festival of Sacrifice |
| | June 11 | Beginning of the Islamic year 1415 |
| | June 20 | Ashura |
| | August 18-19 | Mawlid; Birthday of the Prophet |
| 1995 | February 1 | Beginning of Ramadan |
| | February 26-27 | Night of Power |
| | March 3 | Festival of Breaking the Fast |
| | April 16 | Easter (Western) |
| | April 23 | Easter (Eastern) |
| | May 10 | Festival of Sacrifice |
| | May 31 | Beginning of the Islamic year 1416 |
| | June 9 | Ashura |
| | August 8-9 | Mawlid; Birthday of the Prophet |
| 1996 | January 21 | Beginning of Ramadan |
| | February 15-16 | Night of Power |
| | February 20 | Festival of Breaking the Fast |
| | April 7 | Easter (Western) |
| | April 14 | Easter (Eastern) |

|      | April 28        | Festival of Sacrifice                      |
|------|-----------------|--------------------------------------------|
|      | May 19          | Beginning of the Islamic year 1417         |
|      | May 28          | Ashura                                     |
|      | July 27-28      | Mawlid; Birthday of the Prophet            |
| 1997 | January 10      | Beginning of Ramadan                       |
|      | February 4-5    | Night of Power                             |
|      | February 9      | Festival of Breaking the Fast              |
|      | March 30        | Easter (Western)                           |
|      | April 18        | Festival of Sacrifice                      |
|      | April 27        | Easter (Eastern)                           |
|      | May 9           | Beginning of the Islamic year 1418         |
|      | May 18          | Ashura                                     |
|      | July 16-17      | Mawlid; Birthday of the Prophet            |
|      | December 31     | Beginning of Ramadan                       |
| 1998 | January 25-26   | Night of Power                             |
|      | January 29      | Festival of Breaking the Fast              |
|      | April 7         | Festival of Sacrifice                      |
|      | April 12        | Easter (Western)                           |
|      | April 19        | Easter (Eastern)                           |
|      | April 27        | Beginning of the Islamic year 1419         |
|      | May 6           | Ashura                                     |
|      | July 5-6        | Mawlid; Birthday of the Prophet            |
|      | December 20     | Beginning of Ramadan                       |
| 1999 | January 14-15   | Night of Power                             |
|      | January 19      | Festival of Breaking the Fast              |
|      | March 28        | Festival of Sacrifice                      |
|      | April 4         | Easter (Western)                           |
|      | April 11        | Easter (Eastern)                           |
|      | April 17        | Beginning of the Islamic year 1420         |
|      | April 26        | Ashura                                     |
|      | June 25-26      | Mawlid; Birthday of the Prophet            |
|      | December 9      | Beginning of Ramadan                       |
| 2000 | January 3-4     | Night of Power                             |
|      | January 8       | Festival of Breaking the Fast              |
|      | March 16        | Festival of Sacrifice                      |
|      | April 6         | Beginning of the Islamic year 1421         |
|      | April 15        | Ashura                                     |

|      | April 23 | Easter (Western) |
|------|----------|------------------|
|      | April 30 | Easter (Western) |
|      | June 14-15 | Mawlid; Birthday of the Prophet |
|      | November 26 | Beginning of Ramadan |
|      | December 21-22 | Night of Power |
|      | December 26 | Festival of Breaking the Fast |
| 2001 | March 5 | Festival of Sacrifice |
|      | March 26 | Beginning of the Islamic year 1422 |
|      | April 4 | Ashura |
|      | April 15 | Easter (Western) |
|      | April 15 | Easter (Eastern) |
|      | June 4 | Mawlid; Birthday of the Prophet |
|      | November 16 | Beginning of Ramadan |
|      | December 16 | Festival of Breaking the Fast |
| 2002 | February 22 | Festival of Sacrifice |
|      | March 15 | Beginning of the Islamic Year 1423 |
|      | March 24 | Ashura |
|      | March 31 | Easter (Western) |
|      | May 2 | Easter (Eastern) |
|      | May 24 | Mawlid; Birthday of the Prophet |
|      | November 6 | Beginning of Ramadan |
|      | December 5 | Festival of Breaking the Fast |
| 2003 | February 11 | Festival of Sacrifice |
|      | March 4 | Beginning of Islamic Year 1424 |
|      | March 13 | Ashura |
|      | April 20 | Easter (Western) |
|      | April 27 | Easter (Eastern) |
|      | May 14 | Mawlid; Birthday of the Prophet |
|      | October 27 | Beginning of Ramadan |
|      | November 25 | Festival of Breaking the Fast |
| 2004 | February 1 | Festival of Sacrifice |
|      | February 21 | Beginning of the Islamic year 1425 |
|      | March 1 | Ashura |
|      | April 11 | Easter (Western) |
|      | April 11 | Easter (Eastern) |
|      | May 2 | Mawlid; Birthday of the Prophet |
|      | October 15 | Beginning of Ramadan |

|      | November 14  | Festival of Breaking the Fast          |
|------|--------------|----------------------------------------|
| 2005 | January 21   | Festival of Sacrifice                  |
|      | February 10  | Beginning of the Islamic year 1426     |
|      | February 19  | Ashura                                 |
|      | March 27     | Easter (Western)                       |
|      | May 1        | Easter (Eastern)                       |
|      | April 21     | Mawlid; Birthday of the Prophet        |
|      | October 4    | Beginning of Ramadan                   |
|      | November 3   | Festival of Breaking the Fast          |
| 2006 | January 10   | Festival of Sacrifice                  |
|      | January 31   | Beginning of the Islamic year 1427     |
|      | February 9   | Ashura                                 |
|      | April 10     | Mawlid; Birthday of the Prophet        |
|      | April 16     | Easter (Western)                       |
|      | April 23     | Easter (Eastern)                       |
|      | September 24 | Beginning of Ramadan                   |
|      | October 23   | Festival of Breaking the Fast          |
|      | December 31  | Festival of Sacrifice                  |
| 2007 | January 20   | Beginning of the Islamic year 1428     |
|      | January 29   | Ashura                                 |
|      | March 31     | Mawlid; Birthday of the Prophet        |
|      | April 8      | Easter (Western)                       |
|      | April 8      | Easter (Eastern)                       |
|      | September 13 | Beginning of Ramadan                   |
|      | October 12   | Festival of Breaking the Fast          |
|      | December 20  | Festival of Sacrifice                  |
| 2008 | January 10   | Beginning of the Islamic year 1429     |
|      | January 19   | Ashura                                 |
|      | March 20     | Mawlid; Birthday of the Prophet        |
|      | March 23     | Easter (Western)                       |
|      | April 27     | Easter (Eastern)                       |
|      | September 1  | Beginning of Ramadan                   |
|      | September 30 | Festival of Breaking the Fast          |
|      | December 8   | Festival of Sacrifice                  |
|      | December 29  | Beginning of the Islamic year 1430     |
| 2009 | January 7    | Ashura                                 |
|      | March 9      | Mawlid; Birthday of the Prophet        |

|      | April 12 | Easter (Western) |
|------|----------|------------------|
|      | April 19 | Easter (Eastern) |
|      | August 21 | Beginning of Ramadan |
|      | September 20 | Festival of Breaking the Fast |
|      | November 27 | Festival of Sacrifice |
|      | December 18 | Beginning of the Islamic year 1431 |
|      | December 27 | Ashura |
| 2010 | February 26 | Mawlid; Birthday of the Prophet |
|      | April 4 | Easter (Western) |
|      | April 4 | Easter (Eastern) |
|      | August 11 | Beginning of Ramadan |
|      | September 9 | Festival of Breaking the Fast |
|      | November 16 | Festival of Sacrifice |
|      | December 7 | Beginning of Islamic year 1432 |
|      | December 16 | Ashura |

# Index and Glossary
## of Terms

This index is intended to be used together with the contents page: A few terms listed there are not repeated here. The common English spellings, most based on the *New Encyclopaedia Brittanica*, are followed by alternative forms in parentheses.

# Index of Qur'an Passages

# Index of Biblical Passages

## OLD TESTAMENT

## NEW TESTAMENT

# Brief Bibliography
## on Islam

Note: Books regarded as most basic and particularly helpful for the beginner are identified with an asterisk.

## BOOKS

### The Qur'an

Ali, Abdullah Yusuf. *The Holy Qur'an*. Rev. ed. Brentwood, Md.: Amana Corporation for Islamic Propagation Centre International, 1991. Translation of the Qur'an used most widely by mosques in North America; available at Islamic book outlets, Islamic centers, and mosques.

Arberry, Arthur J. *The Koran Interpreted*. New York: Macmillan, 1964. Translation of the Qur'an in elegant English.

*The Challenge of the Scriptures: The Bible and the Qur'an*. Trans. from the French by Stuart E. Brown. Maryknoll, N.Y.: Orbis Books, 1989.

Cragg, Kenneth. *The Event of the Qur'an.* London: George Allen &
    Unwin, 1971.
_____. *The Mind of the Qur'an.* London: George Allen &
    Unwin, 1973.
*_____, ed. and trans. *Readings in the Qur'an.* London: Collins
    Liturgical Publications, 1988.
Kassis, Hanna E. *A Concordance of the Qur'an.* Berkeley: University
    of California Press, 1983.
Kheri, Al-haj Khan Bahadur Altaf Ahmad. *A Key to the Holy Qur'an:
    Index-cum-Concordance for the Holy Qur'an.* Vol. 1. Karachi, Pak-
    istan: Holy Qur'an Society of Pakistan, 1974. A helpful if cum-
    bersome guide for identifying the location of many words,
    subjects, and Arabic terms in the Qur'an.
Pickthall, Mohammed Marmaduke. *The Meaning of the Glorious Ko-
    ran.* New York: Dover Publications, 1977. Popular translation
    of the Qur'an.
Sherif, Faruq. *A Guide to the Contents of the Qur'an.* London: Ithaca
    Press, 1985.
Watt, W. Montgomery. *Bell's Introduction to the Qur'an.* Rev. ed.
    Edinburgh: Edinburgh University Press, 1970.

## Muhammad

Andrae, Tor. *Muhammed, the Man and His Faith.* Trans. from the
    German. London: George Allen and Unwin, 1956.
Cragg, Kenneth. *Muhammad and the Christian: A Question of Response.*
    Maryknoll, N.Y.: Orbis Books, 1984.
Watt, W. Montgomery. *Muhammad: at Mecca.* London: Oxford Uni-
    versity Press, 1953.
_____. *Muhammad: at Medina.* London: Oxford University
    Press, 1956.
_____. *Muhammad: Prophet and Statesman.* London: Oxford Uni-
    versity Press, 1961.

## Introductions to Islamic History, Culture, and Thought

*Denny, Frederick M. *An Introduction to Islam.* New York: Macmillan,
    1985. Major introductory study by a fine scholar.

*Esposito, John L. *Islam: The Straight Path.* New York: Oxford University Press, 1988. Useful introduction emphasizing contemporary developments.

Guillaume, Alfred. *The Traditions of Islam: An Introduction to the Study of the Hadith Literature.* Oxford: Oxford University Press, 1924.

Glasse, Cyril. *The Concise Encyclopedia of Islam.* San Francisco: Harper & Row, 1989.

Grunebaum, G. E. von. *Muhammadan Festivals.* New York: Henry Schuman, 1951.

Haddad, Yvonne Yazbeck, John Obert Voll, and John L. Esposito, with Kathleen Moore and David Sawan, eds. *The Contemporary Islamic Revival: A Critical Survey and Bibliography.* Bibliographies and Indexes in Religious Studies, no. 20. Westport, Conn.: Greenwood Press, 1991.

*Haneef, Suzanne. *What Everyone Should Know about Islam and Muslims.* Des Plaines, Ill: Library of Islam (P.O. Box 1923), 1985. Helpful guide by an American Christian convert to Islam.

Hitti, Philip K. *History of the Arabs.* New York: St. Martin's Press, 1970.

Hodgson, Marshall G. S. *The Venture of Islam: Conscience and History in a World Civilization.* 3 vols. Chicago: University of Chicago Press, 1974. Comprehensive and erudite study of Islam throughout history.

Holt, P. M., Ann K. S. Lambton, and Bernard Lewis, eds. *The Cambridge History of Islam.* 4 vols. Cambridge: Cambridge University Press, 1970.

Levy, Reuben. *The Social Structure of Islam.* Cambridge: Cambridge University Press, 1957.

Lewis, Bernard. *Islam: From the Prophet Muhammad to the Capture of Constantinople.* 2 vols. New York: Harper & Row, 1974.

Martin, Richard C. *Islam: A Cultural Perspective.* Englewood Cliffs, N.J.: Prentice-Hall, 1982. Brief general introduction.

Mernissi, Fatima. *The Veil and the Male Elite: A Feminist Interpretation of Women's Rights in Islam.* Trans. Mary Jo Lakeland. Reading, Mass.: Addison-Wesley, 1991.

Murata, Sachiko. *The Tao of Islam: A Sourcebook on Gender Relationships in Islamic Thought.* Albany: State University of New York Press, 1992.

Padwick, Constance E. *Muslim Devotions: A Study of Prayer-Manuals in Common Use.* London: SPCK, 1961.

Rahman, Fazlur. *Islam.* Garden City, N.Y.: Anchor Books, 1966. Standard introduction by a Muslim scholar.

*————. *Major Themes of the Qur'an.* Minneapolis: Bibliotheca Islamica, 1980. Excellent introduction to a modern Muslim theological interpretation of the Qur'anic message.

Schacht, J., and Bosworth Schacht, eds. *The Legacy of Islam.* 2d ed. Oxford: Oxford University Press, 1974.

Schimmel, Annemarie. *Mystical Dimensions of Islam.* Chapel Hill: University of North Carolina Press, 1978.

Smith, Wilfred Cantwell. *Islam in Modern History.* Princeton, N.J.: Princeton University Press, 1957.

*Speight, R. Marston. *God Is One: The Way of Islam.* New York: Friendship Press, 1989. Brief introduction for Christians.

Trimingham, J. Spencer. *The Sufi Orders in Islam.* Oxford: Oxford University Press, 1971.

Watt, W. Montgomery. *The Formative Period of Islamic Thought.* Edinburgh: Edinburgh University Press, 1973.

Weekes, Richard V., ed. *Muslim Peoples: A World Ethnographic Survey.* Westport, Conn.: Greenwood Press, 1978.

## Reference Resources

Adams, Charles J., ed. *A Reader's Guide to the Great Religions.* New York: Free Press, 1977.

Arnold, T. W., et al., eds. *First Encyclopaedia of Islam 1913–1936.* Reprint. Leiden: E. J. Brill, 1987.

Brice, William C., ed. *An Historical Atlas of Islam.* Leiden: E. J. Brill, 1981.

Ede, David, ed. *Guide to Islam.* Boston: G. K. Hall & Co., 1983.

Eliade, Mircea, ed. *The Encyclopedia of Religion.* New York: Macmillan, 1987. See vol. 7, pp. 303–464 (also see index).

Faruqi, Isma'il R. al, and Lois Lamya'al Faruqi. *The Cultural Atlas of Islam.* New York: Macmillan, 1986.

Geddes, Charles L. *An Analytical Guide to the Bibliographies on Islam, Muhammad, and the Qur'an.* Denver: American Institute of Islamic Studies, 1973.

_____. *Books in English on Islam, Muhammad, and the Qur'an.* Denver: American Institute of Islamic Studies, 1976.

*Gibb, H. A. R., and J. H. Kramers, eds. *Shorter Encyclopaedia of Islam.* Leiden: E. J. Brill, 1953. A standard reference.

*Gibb, H. A. R., J. H. Kramers, E. Levi-Provencal, J. Schacht, et al., eds. *The Encyclopedia of Islam.* New ed. Leiden: E. J. Brill, 1960–. The most complete multivolume encyclopedia, still in the process of writing and publication.

Pearson, J. D., ed. *Index Islamicus (Guide to Periodical Literature, 1906–1970).* Cambridge, England: W. Heffner and Sons, Ltd., 1972.

Robinson, Francis. *Atlas of the Islamic World Since 1500.* New York: Facts on File, 1982.

Verhoeven, F. R. J. *Islam, Its Origin and Spread in Words, Maps and Pictures.* Amsterdam: Djambatan, 1962.

## Christianity and Islam

Abdul-Haqq, Abdiyah Akbar. *Sharing Your Faith with a Muslim.* Minneapolis: Bethany Fellowship, 1980.

Addison, James T. *The Christian Approach to the Moslem: A Historical Study.* New York: Columbia University Press, 1942.

Bentley, David, ed. *Rights of Muslims: A Scale for Christian Understanding of Religious Tolerance in 33 Muslim Majority Nations in 1991.* Pasadena, Calif: Zwemer Institute of Muslim Studies,1992.

*Christians Meeting Muslims. WCC Papers on Ten Years of Christian-Muslim Dialogue.* Geneva: World Council of Churches, 1977.

Cohn-Sherbok, Dan, ed. *Islam in a World of Diverse Faiths.* New York: St. Martin's Press, 1991.

*Cragg, Kenneth. *The Call of the Minaret.* London: Oxford University Press, 1964. Now-classic treatment of the subject.

Daniel, N. A. *Islam and the West: The Making of an Image.* Edinburgh: Edinburgh University Press, 1960.

Dretke, James P. *A Christian Approach to Muslims: Reflections from West Africa.* Pasadena, Calif: William Carey Library, 1979.

Falaturi, Abdoldjavad, and Annemarie Schimmel, eds. *We Believe in One God: The Experience of God in Christianity and Islam.* New York: Seabury Press, 1979.

Haines, Byron L., and Frank L. Cooley, eds. *Christians and Muslims Together: An Exploration by Presbyterians*. Philadelphia: Geneva Press, 1987.

*Kateregga, Badru D., and David W. Shenk. *Islam and Christianity*. Grand Rapids, Mich.: Eerdmans, 1981. Very basic presentation of the teachings of each religion by believers.

Lochhaas, Philip H. *How to Respond to . . . Islam*. Rev. ed. St. Louis: Concordia Publishing House, 1990. A brief booklet (32 pp.).

McCurry, Don, ed. *The Gospel and Islam: A 1978 Compendium*. Monrovia, Calif.: MARC, 1979.

Miller, William M. *A Christian's Response to Islam*. Wheaton, Ill.: Tyndale House, 1980.

———. *Ten Muslims Meet Christ*. Grand Rapids, Mich.: Eerdmans, 1969.

Parrinder, Geoffrey. *Jesus in the Qur'an*. 2d ed. London: Sheldon Press, 1976.

*Parshall, Phil. *New Paths in Muslim Evangelism*. Grand Rapids, Mich.: Baker Book House, 1980.

Rajashekar, J. Paul, ed. *Christian-Muslim Relations in Eastern Africa*. Geneva: Lutheran World Federation, 1988. Report of a seminar/workshop sponsored by the LWF and the Project for Christian-Muslim Relations in Africa, Nairobi, 2–8 May 1987.

Rajashekar, J. Paul, and H. S. Wilson, eds. *Islam in Asia: Perspectives for Christian-Muslim Encounter*. Geneva: Lutheran World Federation, 1992. Report of a consultation sponsored by the LWF and the World Alliance of Reformed Churches, Bangkok, 11–15 June 1991.

*Thomsen, Mark. *God and Jesus: Theological Reflections for Christian-Muslim Dialogue*. Minneapolis: ALC, 1986. A Lutheran contribution.

Vander Werff, Lyle L. *Christian Mission to Muslims—The Record, Anglican and Reformed Approaches in India and the Near East, 1800–1938*. Pasadena, Calif: William Carey Library, 1977.

Watt, William Montgomery. *Muslim-Christian Encounters: Perceptions and Misperceptions*. New York: Routledge, 1991.

Woodbury, Dudley, ed. *Muslims and Christians on the Emmaus Road*. Monrovia, Calif.: MARC 1989.

Ye'or, Bat. *The Dhimmi: Jews and Christians under Islam.* Trans. from the French by David Maisel, Paul Fenton, and David Littman. Rutherford, N.J.: Fairleigh Dickinson University Press, 1985.

## Islam in the United States

Abraham, Sameer Y., and Nabeel Abraham, eds. *Arabs in the New World: Studies on Arab-American Communities.* Detroit: Wayne State University, Center for Urban Studies, 1983.

Al-Faruqi, Ism'ail R. "Islamic Ideals in North America." In *The Muslim Community in North America,* ed. Earle H. Waugh et al., 259–70. Edmonton: University of Alberta Press, 1983.

Austin, Allan D. *African Muslims in Antebellum America: A Sourcebook.* Critical Studies on Black Life and Culture, vol. 5. New York: Garland, 1984.

Blyden, Edward Wilmot. *Christianity, Islam and the Negro Race.* London: W. B. Whittingham & Co., 1888.

Green, Betty Patchin. "The Alcaldes of California." *Aramco World Magazine* (Nov.–Dec. 1976): 26–29.

Haddad, Yvonne Yazbeck. "Arab Muslims and Islamic Institutions in America: Adaptation and Reform." In *Arabs in the New World: Studies on Arab-American Communities,* ed. Sameer Y. Abraham and Nabeel Abraham, 65–81. Detroit: Wayne State University, Center for Urban Studies, 1983.

———. "Muslims in America: A Select Bibliography." *The Muslim World* 76 (1986): 93–122.

———. "The Muslim Experience in the United States." *The Link* 2:4 (Sept.–Oct. 1979): 1–11.

———. "Muslims in the United States." In *Islam: The Religious and Political Life of a World Community,* ed. Marjorie Kelly, 258–74. New York: Praeger, 1984.

*———, ed. *Mission to America: Five Islamic Sectarian Communities in North America.* Gainesville: University Press of Florida, 1993.

*———, ed. *The Muslims of America.* New York: Oxford University Press, 1991.

*Haddad, Yvonne Yazbeck, and Adair T. Lummis. *Islamic Values in the United States.* New York: Oxford University Press, 1987.

Haddad, Yvonne Yazbeck, Byron Haines, and Ellison Findly, eds. *The Islamic Impact.* Syracuse, N.Y.: Syracuse University Press, 1984.

*Haddad, Yvonne Yazbeck, and Jane Smith, eds. *The Muslim Community in the United States.* New York: State University of New York Press, 1994.

Haddad, Yvonne Yazbeck, John Obert Voll, and John L. Esposito, with Kathleen Moore and David Sawan, eds. *The Contemporary Islamic Revival: A Critical Survey and Bibliography.* Bibliographies and Indexes in Religious Studies, no. 20. New York: Greenwood Press, 1991.

Haley, Alex, and Malcolm X. *The Autobiography of Malcolm X.* New York: Grove Press, 1966.

Kelly, Marjorie, ed. *Islam: The Religious and Political Life of a World Community.* New York: Praeger, 1984. See pp. 258–74.

Koszegi, Michael A., and J. Gordon Melton. *Islam in North America: A Sourcebook.* Religious Information Systems, no 8. New York: Garland Publishing, 1992.

Lincoln, C. Eric. "The American Muslim Mission in the Context of American Social History." In *The Muslim Community in North America*, ed. Earle H. Waugh et al., 215–33. Edmonton: University of Alberta Press, 1983.

———. *The Black Muslims in America.* Boston: Beacon Press, 1961.

Lovell, Emily Kalled. "Islam in the United States: Past and Present." In *The Muslim Community in North America*, ed. Earle H. Waugh, et al., 93–110. Edmonton: University of Alberta Press, 1983.

Makdisi, Nadim. "The Moslems in America." *The Christian Century* 76:34 (26 Aug. 1959): 969–71.

Mallon, Elias. *Neighbors: Muslims in North America.* New York: Friendship Press, 1989.

Mamiya, Lawrence H. "Minister Louis Farrakhan and the Final Call: Schism in the Muslim Movement." In *The Muslim Community in North America*, ed. Earle H. Waugh, et al., 234–55. Edmonton: University of Alberta Press, 1983.

Mehdi, Beverlee Turner, ed. *The Arabs in America 1492–1977: A Chronology and Fact Book.* Dobbs Ferry, N.Y.: Oceana Publications, 1978.

Meir, Aryeh, and Reuven Firestone. *Islam in America*. New York: American Jewish Committee, Institute of Human Relations, 1992.

Miller, Deborah L. "Middle Easterners: Syrians, Lebanese, Armenians, Egyptians, Iranians, Palestinians, Turks, Afghans." In *They Chose Minnesota: A Survey of the State's Ethnic Groups*, ed. June Drenning Holmquist, 511–30. St. Paul: Minnesota Historical Society Press, 1981.

Moore, Kathleen. "Muslims in Prison: Claims to Constitutional Protection of Religious Liberty." In *The Muslims of America*, ed. Yvonne Yazbeck Haddad, 136–56. New York: Oxford University Press, 1991.

Poston, Larry Allan. "Da'wa in the West." In *The Muslims of America*, ed. Yvonne Yazbeck Haddad, 125–35. New York: Oxford University Press, 1991.

———. *Islamic Da'wah in the West: Muslim Missionary Activity and the Dynamics of Conversion to Islam*. New York: Oxford University Press, 1992.

Richardson, E. Allen. *Islamic Churches in North America: Patterns of Belief and Devotion of Muslims from Asian Countries in the United States and Canada*. New York: Pilgrim Press, 1981.

Speight, R. Marston. *Christian-Muslim Relations: An Introduction for Christians in the United States of America*. Hartford: Task Force on Christian-Muslim Relations, National Council of the Churches of Christ in the USA, 1983.

*Statistical Abstract of the United States*. Washington, D.C.: Bureau of Census, Department of Commerce, 1987.

Stone, Carol L. "Estimate of Muslims Living in America." In *The Muslims of America*, ed. Yvonne Yazbeck Haddad, 25–36. New York: Oxford University Press, 1991.

Thernsten, Stephan, ed. *Harvard Encyclopedia of American Ethnic Groups*. Cambridge, Mass.: Harvard University Press, 1980.

Voll, John O. "Islamic Issues for Muslims in the United States." In *The Muslims of America*, ed. Yvonne Yazbeck Haddad, 205–16. New York: Oxford University Press, 1991.

Waugh, Earle H. "Imam in the New World: Models and Modifications." In *Transitions and Transformations in the History of*

*Religions*, ed. Frank E. Reynolds and Theodore M. Ludwig, 124–49.Leiden: E. J. Brill, 1980.

———. "Muslim Leadership and the Shaping of the Umma: Classical Tradition and Religious Tension in the North American Setting." In *The Muslim Community in North America*, ed. Earle H. Waugh et al., 11–33. Edmonton: University of Alberta Press, 1983.

Waugh, Earle H., Baha Abu-Laban, and Regula B. Qureshi, eds. *The Muslim Community in North America*. Edmonton: University of Alberta Press, 1983.

Winters, Clyde-Ahmad. "Afro-American Muslims from Slavery to Freedom." *Islamic Studies* 17:4 (1978): 187–205.

Women's Committee of the MSA. *Parents' Manual: A Guide for Muslim Parents Living in North America*. Brentwood, Md.: American Trust Publications, 1976.

## JOURNALS

*al-Ittihad* (Muslim Students' Association of the United States and Canada, Plainfield, Ind.)

*al-Mushir* (The Counselor, theological journal of the Christian Study Centre, Rawalpindi, West Pakistan)

*The American Muslim Journal* (formerly the *Muslim Journal* and before that *Muhammad Speaks*, and before that again *Bilalian News*; publication of the American Muslim Mission

*International Bulletin of Missionary Research* (Overseas Ministries Study Center, New Haven, Conn.)

*Islamic Horizons* (Muslim Students' Association of the United States and Canada, Plainfield, Ind.)

*Islamochristiana* (Rome)

*Journal of Near Eastern Studies* (Chicago)

*The International Review of Mission* (Geneva, World Council of Churches; with current bibliographies)

*The Link* (publication of Americans for Middle East Understanding, Inc.)

*The Middle East Journal* (Middle East Institute, Washington, D.C.)

*Missiology* (American Society of Missiology, Elkhart, Ind.)

*Missionalia* (South African Missiological Society, Pretoria, South Africa)

*\*The Muslim World* (Hartford; with extensive current bibliographies)

*Newsletter for Christian-Muslim Concerns* (publication of Office of Christian-Muslim Concerns, National Council of Christian Churches in the USA)

# Organizations

(Useful resources may be acquired from many of these.)

## 1. MUSLIM

American Muslim Mission
    Masjid Hon. Elijah Muhammad
    7351 S. Stony Island Ave.
    Chicago, IL 60649
    (312) 643-0700

American Muslim Council
    1212 New York Ave. NW, Suite 525
    Washington, DC 20005
    (202) 789-2262
        (A coordinating body for Islamic groups in their relations
        with other religious communities and the government)

Federation of Islamic Associations in the USA and Canada, Inc.
    17514 Woodward
    Detroit, MI 48203
    (313) 849-2147

Institute of Islamic Information and Education (III&E)
    4390 N. Elston Ave.
    Chicago, IL 60641
    (312) 777-7443

International Institute of Islamic Thought
    P.O. Box 669
    555 Grove St.
    Herndon, VA 22070
    (703) 471-1133, FAX (703) 471-3922

Iqra' International Education Foundation
    831 S. Lafallin
    Chicago, IL 60607
    (312) 226-5694, FAX (312) 226-4125

Islamic Book Service
    10900 W. Washington St.
    Indianapolis, IN 46231
    (317) 839-8150

Islamic Center of Washington, DC
    2551 Massachusetts Ave. NW
    Washington, DC 20008
    (202) 332-8343
        (Publishes a free quarterly journal in English, *Al Nur* [The
        Light])

Islamic Society of North America
    Box 38
    Plainfield, IN 46168
    (317) 839-8157, (317) 839-1811

(This is also the national offices of Muslim Students' Association. ISNA provides a 90 + -page booklet listing Islamic centers, schools, mosques (Masajid), MSA chapters, and Islamic media organizations in cities throughout the United States.)

*Muslim Journal*
910 W. Van Buren, Suite 100
Chicago, IL 60607
(312) 243-7600
(Published under leadership of Warith Deen.)

Muslim World League Office of North America
134 W. 26th St., 11th floor
New York, NY 10001
(212) 627-4033
(International headquarters is P.O. Box 537, Mecca, Saudi Arabia)

Nation of Islam
Louis Farrakhan
4855 S. Woodlawn Ave.
Chicago, IL 60615
(312) 324-6000
also:
FCN Publishing Company
734 W. 79th St.
Chicago, IL 60620
(312) 602-1230
(Not accepted by Muslims as orthodox. Publishes the periodical *Final Call.*)

## 2. CHRISTIAN

Americans for Middle East Understanding, Inc.
475 Riverside Drive, Room 241

New York, NY 10115
(212) 870-2053, FAX (212) 870-2050

Department of Interfaith Witness, Home Mission Board
Southern Baptist Convention
    1350 Spring Street, NE
    Atlanta, GA 30367
    (404) 873-4041 or (800) 634-2462

Duncan Black Macdonald Center for the Study of Islam and Chris-
    tian-Muslim Relations
Hartford Seminary
    77 Sherman St.
    Hartford, CT 06105
    (203) 232-4451

Islamic Studies Program
Luther Seminary
    2481 Como Ave.
    St. Paul, MN 55108
    (612) 641-3506 (or 3390)

Mission Advanced Research Center (MARC)
World Vision International
    919 West Huntington Drive
    Monrovia, CA 91016-9909
    (818) 301-7703 (Bruce Bradshaw), FAX (818) 301-7786

National Conference of Catholic Bishops
Secretariat for Ecumenical and Interreligious Affairs
    3211 4th St. NE
    Washington, DC 20017
    (202) 541-3025

Office of Christian-Muslim Concerns, NCCC USA
    (see Duncan Black Macdonald Center)

Overseas Ministries Study Center
    490 Prospect St.
    New Haven, CT 06511
    (203) 624-6672, FAX (203) 865-2857

Presbyterian Church USA
Ecumenical and Interfaith Office
    100 Witherspoon St.
    Louisville, KY 40202-1396
    (502) 569-5000, FAX (502) 569-5018

Steering Committee for Consultation of Muslim-Christian Relations
Dr. Harold Vogelar
Lutheran School of Theology
    1100 E. 55th Street
    Chicago, IL 60615
    (312) 753-0700

Zwemer Institute of Islamic Studies
    P.O. Box 41330
    Pasadena, CA 91114
    (818) 794-1121, FAX (818) 798-3469

## 3. INTERFAITH

The National Conference of Christians and Jews
    (and recently including Muslims)
    71 5th Ave.
    New York, NY 10003
    (212) 206-0006

World Conference on Religion and Peace
U.S. Committee
    777 United Nations Plaza, Suite 9A
    New York, NY 10017
    (212) 687-2163, FAX (212) 983-0566

## 4. OTHER

The American Jewish Committee
Institute of Human Relations
165 East 56th Street
New York, NY 10022-2746